The Necropolitical Theater

The Necropolitical Theater

Race and Immigration on the Contemporary Spanish Stage

✦

Jeffrey K. Coleman

NORTHWESTERN UNIVERSITY PRESS
EVANSTON, ILLINOIS

Northwestern University Press
www.nupress.northwestern.edu

Printed in the United States of America

10 9 8 7 6 5 4 3 2 1

Library of Congress Cataloging-in-Publication Data

Names: Coleman, Jeffrey K, author.
Title: The necropolitical theater : race and immigration on the contemporary Spanish stage / Jeffrey K Coleman.
Description: Evanston, Illinois : Northwestern University Press, 2020. | Includes bibliographical references and index
Identifiers: LCCN 2019023582 | ISBN 9780810141858 (paperback) | ISBN 9780810141865 (cloth) | ISBN 9780810141872 (ebook)
Subjects: LCSH: Spanish drama—20th century—History and criticism. | Spanish drama—21st century—History and criticism. | Immigrants in literature. | Race relations in literature. | Death in literature.
Classification: LCC PQ6115 .C64 2020 | DDC 862.64093526912—dc23
LC record available at https://lccn.loc.gov/2019023582

To Ruth and Nellie Mancell, for teaching me to always travel through the world with my eyes and ears wide open to access the stories of those around me.

CONTENTS

ACKNOWLEDGMENTS

Writing one's first book is always a daunting experience. I would add that writing *The Necropolitical Theater* has been an experience of incredible growth for me. Finally finding my voice in the solitude of writing was a difficult feat made possible with the support of a network of people that recognized the power of this work, at times before I could even conceive the words. As such, I want to thank the people and institutions without which this book would still be a dream deferred.

First, I thank Diana Aramburu and N. Michelle Murray for encouraging me to pursue writing this book, despite the pressures of the tenure clock calling me not to start a new project. This book is at its core about pushing against norms, both theatrical and academic.

As the process of book writing is solitary by nature, it was pivotal for me to find intellectual soundboards in and out of my field with whom I could test my ideas. I owe a great deal to Joel Berkowitz, William Viestenz, Ryan Calabretta-Sajder, Martin Repinecz, Harry Karahalios, Anna Tybinko, Sameena Mulla, Noelle Brigden, Ermitte Saint-Jacques, Tara Daly, Eugenia Afinoguénova, Pablo José López Oro, Stuart Green, Glenn García, Matthew Algeo, and Paola Hernández for reading drafts and providing such brilliant feedback.

One of the great joys of this process has been the ability to speak across fields to find the words that Hispanic studies lacks. For that I am eternally grateful to Julius B. Fleming Jr. for introducing me to necropolitics as a theoretical framework through which I found the path to analyze race and immigration in Spain.

Numbers have never been my strong point, but that is why you need a scientist best friend to help you wade through immigration data. Thank you, Martin B. Lee, for enabling me to see patterns across time and for continuously motivating me when I was down. Your support means more than you will ever know.

There are people in your life who cheer you on even when they know they cannot do much to help you in the moment. My grandmother, Nellie Mancell, is my biggest fan and supporter. Thank you for all your prayers and for speaking this book into existence.

This book would not be nearly as strong as it is if not for the book manuscript workshop I hosted on September 28, 2018. Sameena Mulla, you are a godsend for organizing the workshop and for fighting for me when so many others were unsupportive of humanities research on campus. I hope out of your efforts there will be institutional support for humanities scholars in the future.

Research is one of the wonders of our profession and I am grateful to my undergraduate research assistants, Maxwell Moloney and Zoe Campbell, for entering the depths of the archives with me to discover the gems that shine so brightly in this book.

My time in Spain was crucial to be able to access the materials and people necessary to construct the claims that appear in this book. Without the support of the Woodrow Wilson Fellowship Foundation, I would not have had the time and space to conduct the research that made this book possible. Also, the staff at the Centro de Documentación Teatral (Center for Theatrical Documentation) and the Teatre Nacional de Catalunya (National Theater of Catalunya) were pivotal to my gaining access to recordings and reviews of plays, and especially for putting me in touch with playwrights.

I have always been struck by the kindness of the Spanish playwrights who have opened their homes, hearts, and minds to me for interviews and brainstorming. Thank you all for your time and for helping me to love theater even more than I already did.

And finally, to my saint of a partner, Travis Reed, thank you for all the ways you supported me through this entire journey, including the months apart while I was doing archival research and the mock presentations you endured, the paragraphs you listened to, and the many liters of coffee and tea you perfectly brewed for me so I could write.

NOTE ON TRANSLATION

As many of my primary sources are in Spanish, I have included English translations of Spanish quotations for those who are unable to read the original texts. Unless otherwise noted, English translations of all quotations are my own. When an English translation of the entire play I analyze has been published, I cite and note the published translation in addition to the Spanish original.

ABBREVIATIONS

AMNT	*Allegro (ma non troppo)*
AP	*Ataque preventivo* (*Preventive Attack*)
DMG	*Dark Man's Gaze*
DNI	documento nacional de identidad (national identity document)
ETA	Euskadi Ta Askatasuna (Spain's Basque separatist group, Basque Homeland and Freedom)
EU	European Union
FE	(newspaper for Falange Española, Spanish Phalanx party)
INE	Instituto Nacional de Estadística (Spanish Statistical Office)
LFMJN	*La falsa muerte de Jaro el Negro* (*The False Death of Jaro the Negro*)
LMHO	*La mirada del hombre oscuro* (*Dark Man's Gaze*)
LO	*Ley Orgánica* (*Organic Law*)
LVHLC	*Los viernes del Hotel Luna Caribe* (*Fridays at the Caribbean Moon Hotel*)
ML	*Mercado libre* (*Free Market*)
NGO	nongovernmental organization
PRI	Public Radio International
UPV	*Unos pájaros verdes* (*Some Green Birds*)

The Necropolitical Theater

Introduction

✦

The Formation of the Necropolitical Theater

Spain has been dramatically transformed by immigration over the last thirty years. The influx of immigrants since the early 1990s has been described as, among other things, a flood, an avalanche, an invasion, and a seismic phenomenon.[1] These references to natural and military disasters articulate a notion of immigration as a threat to the political and cultural well-being of the Spanish nation-state.[2] During the same time period, Spanish playwrights have written a multitude of plays aimed at helping audiences reach a sociopolitical and affective understanding of the impacts of immigration on their nation. However, many of the plays, despite aiming to humanize the immigrant experience, actually reify the sensationalized, autochthonous anxieties that are often found in the media and in politics.[3] *The Necropolitical Theater: Race and Immigration on the Contemporary Spanish Stage* was born out of a desire to understand what happens once immigration begins and racial formation takes root in a nation, thereby invoking societal anxiety regarding the alleged imminent disaster. More precisely, by interrogating the repercussions of the migratory phenomenon and how they ripple into patterns of theatrical representation, we can reach a deeper understanding of how Spain is imagining and creating race.

The Necropolitical Theater is an examination of Spanish immigration theater from 1991 to 2016, examining plays in which the main plot follows a protagonist's immigration into Spain or the experience of an immigrant already in Spain. The book's temporal scope is anchored on one end by the 1991 play *La mirada del hombre oscuro* (*LMHO*) (*Dark Man's Gaze* [*DMG*]) by Ignacio del Moral, the first play to portray the contemporary immigration phenomenon, and on the other end by 2016, the year in which *Los mares de Caronte: Diecisiete calas dramáticas sobre migraciones* (*The Seas of Charon: Seventeen Short Dramatic Works about Migration*) was published.[4] This collection edited by Concha Fernández Soto and Francisco Checa y Olmos compiles seventeen short theatrical works (or selections of works) that highlight how contemporary playwrights are engaging with the topic of immigration. The collection's title uses Greek mythological imagery in which the ferryman Charon led the souls of the dead across the Rivers Styx and Acheron to reach

Hades. As death is so intertwined with theatrical representations of Spanish immigration, it is only fitting that this collection serve as the temporal bookend to this study. In addition, 2016 marks the year in which Brexit, Trump, and rising Far Right nationalist movements across Europe reinvigorated intense discussions about immigration in Spain, stoking the flames of discussions that have been ongoing since the 1990s, as studied in books on other cultural genres such as those by Rosalía Cornejo-Parriego, Daniela Flesler, Jessica Folkart, and Benita Sampedro Vizcaya, among others. Through this examination of theatrical works, this book underscores the importance of theater in exploring questions of race and national identity by analyzing how Spanish playwrights have portrayed the experiences of three of the nation's main immigrant groups: Latin Americans, North Africans, and sub-Saharan Africans. The ensuing chapters will demonstrate that Spanish immigration theater has a necropolitical genealogy that can be traced back to *La mirada del hombre oscuro*. Therefore, these plays' necropolitics is canonized through its racialized portrayal of the three aforementioned immigrant groups, manifested differently for each group, thereby establishing an inherent racial hierarchy.

Hierarchies of Race

Despite being the largest regional demographic of immigrants to Spain, European citizens (especially from the United Kingdom, Romania, and Germany) have integrated into Spanish society as "expats" rather than "immigrants." The linguistic distinction facilitates the integration of culturally disparate peoples into Spanish society based on the latter's aspiration for whiteness, which "elevates" Spain closer to its European neighbors. As Baltasar Fra-Molinero states, "One of the arguments northern Europeans leveled against Spain and Spaniards was predicated on race. Northern Europeans charged that Spaniards were less than white," as a result of its close cultural ties to Africa grounded in the nearly eight centuries of Islamic presence that existed in the Iberian Peninsula from 711 to 1492.[5] This mentality is distilled into the famous phrase *África empieza en los Pirineos* (Africa begins in the Pyrenees), which implies that Spain is not part of Europe but rather an extension of Africa. For this reason, Spain's push for Europeanization (i.e., its entrance into the European Union [EU]) in the 1980s was not only a maneuver of political and economic integration but also an integration into whiteness, substantiated by entry into Europe's most exclusive supranational club.

When large-scale immigration began in the early 1990s, it signaled a recognition of Spain's successful ascension to whiteness. As Fra-Molinero states: "Spain is white in as much as it receives nonwhite immigrants. Following this equation, the more immigrants it receives, the whiter Spain becomes."[6] The shift from a nation of emigration to a nation of immigration heralds Spain's shift from a nonwhite nation to a European nation—one that is intrinsically white. For this reason, European immigrants to Spain will not be studied in this book, as they do not disrupt Spain's national identity in nearly as dramatic a fashion as nonwhite immigrant groups do. The decision to focus on Latin Americans, North Africans, and sub-Saharan Africans is therefore predicated on their being the largest nonwhite immigrant groups with a longstanding history in Spain. In addition, they also are the groups about which the most immigration plays have been written and staged.[7]

The Necropolitics of Immigration in Spain

As the theoretical base on which to construct the arguments that will follow in the chapters to come, I employ Achille Mbembe's concept of necropolitics to demonstrate that the theatrical representation of these three major migrant groups in Spain (Latin Americans, North Africans, and sub-Saharan Africans) delineates the construction of a racial hierarchy encompassing social marginalization, forced assimilation, and in the most extreme cases, physical death. As Mbembe outlines, "the ultimate expression of sovereignty resides, to a large degree, in the power and the capacity to dictate who may live and who must die."[8] This power, which is not always wielded by the state itself, may be wielded by individuals or institutions that support and wish to uphold state ideals of sovereignty, which "continuously refers and appeals to exception, emergency, and a fictionalized notion of the enemy. It also labors to produce that same exception, emergency, and fictionalized enemy" (16). In this book, I focus on the production of the fictionalized enemy: the creation of a narrative that portrays immigrants as inimical and antithetical to Spanish society. As theater transmits sociopolitical messages, the didactic nature of Spanish immigration plays then constitutes what I call necropolitical theater wherein the immigrant is transformed into the fictionalized enemy whose nonwhiteness is incompatible with Spanish society and national identity, and therefore a threat to the (European) Spanish state. The necropolitical representation of the relationship between Spain and its immigrant groups facilitates an understanding of how the quickly evolving demographics are developing and teaching racial knowledge that ultimately promotes a theater of whiteness. Death of the immigrant not only "purifies" Spain by portraying the maintenance of the status quo but also provides the moment of catharsis for the spectator faced with the notion of a racially diverse nation.

This study will expose the necropolitical nature of Spanish theater by looking collectively at the corpus of plays instead of exploring the merits of individual plays. When analyzed in relation to the corpus, plays intended to develop humanizing immigrant narratives have actually formed a canon that concenters around the failure and death of the immigrant. Through the use of problematic tropes and stereotypes, these plays canonize necropolitical racial thinking that continues to affect how issues of race and identity are portrayed on the contemporary Spanish stage.

Although necropolitics is centered on death as the cornerstone of sovereignty, this death need not be a physical one. There are cases in which the state, state actors, or individuals benefit from maintaining the Other as a member of the living dead, which Mbembe and Meintjes describe as a "slave condition [that] results from a triple loss: loss of a 'home,' loss of rights over his or her body, and loss of political status. This triple loss is identical with absolute domination, natal alienation, and social death (expulsion from humanity altogether)" (21). This triple loss constitutes a zombie status that I will later refer to as "necropolitical captivity," a condition in which the immigrant is relegated to a social death via marginalization and ostracism.[9] My concept of necropolitical captivity is equally informed by Lisa Marie Cacho's explication of social death, which is useful for understanding how race is weaponized against people of color, to the extent that their very existence becomes a threat to be tamed. She notes, "human value is made intelligible through racialized, sexualized, spatialized, and state-sponsored violences."[10] If the threat of violence is a constant fear for nonwhite immigrants, then social death via forced assimilation, surveillance, or captivity is a necropolitical reality characterized by perpetual violence and trauma from which physical death would provide a compassionate relief. This violent persistence is symbolic of the fact that, as Adrián Pérez-Melgosa asserts, "the human body [functions] as the location where power struggles are staged."[11] Consequently, the staging of the power struggles between autochthonous people and immigrants are corporally performed in Spanish immigration theater as a reflection of those same struggles occurring off stage in Spanish society.

The Case for Theater

Although immigration stories are being told in films, novels, and other genres, this book focuses solely on theater because of the ways this genre uniquely represents the drama of immigration in Spain. The corporeal nature of theater creates a microcosm of society by encapsulating its audience in a fabricated time and space, for theater, unlike other genres, cannot be stopped, nor can it be repeated. As Peter Sellars notes in the foreword to Emma Cox's *Theatre and Migration*: "The act of making theater is the act of recognizing, affirming, extending, imagining, and re-affirming a community or, possibly, communities. Metaphorically at first, and then literally and tangibly, theater is the creation of newly shared space on Earth."[12] The imperfection and singularity of theatrical performance and its audience facilitates an affective experience as unique as one's own migration. The intrinsically ephemeral nature of theater thus creates a sense of urgency that other genres cannot, thereby establishing a gravitas that facilitates the transmission of these didactic (and in this case, necropolitical) messages. In Cox's view, "As such, theatre of migration is at its most basic level implicated with, and troubled by, power relations within the broader society" (27). In this way, theater of migration simultaneously plays on the power dynamics between the spectator and the story being told (i.e., "Is it by/about *them* or is it by/about *us*?"), as well as the dynamics between immigrant and autochthonous characters on stage (27).

There is a surprisingly large archive of more than sixty plays that directly delve into the so-called Spanish immigration question. Yet despite the significantly greater number of theatrical works than films and prose that focus on immigration themes in Spain, there has been little to no academic criticism and analysis of these plays. To date, there has only been one book-length study on the representation of immigration in Spanish theater, Eileen J. Doll's *Los inmigrantes en la escena española contemporánea: Buscando una nueva identidad española* (*Immigrants on the Contemporary Spanish Stage: Searching for a New Spanish Identity*).[13] While comprehensive in regard to the number of plays it analyzes, the book primarily focuses on technical aspects (lighting, music, language, costume design) featured and heavily ignores race as a lens of analysis. Consequently, there is an inability to constellate the systematic patterns that are formed across plays and, in turn, these plays are presented as singular occurrences rather than pieces within a theatrical canon. The present study foregrounds race to critique hegemonic whiteness in the arts, as typified by the work of white, Spanish playwrights. Given the structures of access required to stage a play, it comes as no surprise that there are currently very few nonwhite Spanish playwrights that have been able to stage their perspectives. These minority perspectives are rather seen in novels, essays, and poetry. As Cox notes, "None is owed a moral monopoly on the use of migration as a dramatic trope, but there can be different interests at work when 'outsiders' are written and performed into being by 'insiders,' as contrasted with 'outsiders' enacting some kind of self-representation."[14] One could speculate that the lack of minority perspectives within the interconnectedness of the Spanish theater circuit (i.e., the playwrights, directors, and actors that flow through and into theater schools, theater festivals, and selection juries for dramaturgy prizes) engenders some of the problematic structural patterns I outline throughout the book. To this point, it is worth mentioning that dramaturgy prize committees have consistently awarded prizes to plays that depict stories about immigration, starting with Ignacio del Moral's *La mirada del hombre oscuro*, which won the Premio SGAE in 1991. It is then customary for the winner of the prize to sit on the jury the following year, which allows that playwright's dramaturgical perspective to influence how the prize is awarded in the future. Given this structure, it can be said that by awarding top dramaturgy prizes to immigration plays that promote a necropolitical agenda, these juries are canonizing Spanish epistemologies of race and multiculturalism.

There can be dangerous, unintended consequences when immigration plays aim to humanize the difficulty of immigrants' lived experiences. As Pérez-Melgosa notes in regard to migration films, "[those] whose primary aim may have been to denounce the abuses and injustices suffered by migrants end up participating in a long-ranging form of slow cultural violence that reduces their agency until it renders migrants exclusively into victimized subjects."[15] The same pattern appears in Spanish immigration theater. In my interviews with playwrights, most claim that their objective for writing their respective immigration play was to humanize immigrant experiences. As this book demonstrates, however, these plays develop and contribute to dangerous canonical patterns that impede a positive conceptualization of immigrants and immigration. This canonization is made possible by the dramaturgy prize system that has consistently awarded plays that espouse this "humanizing" narrative. My critique does not discount the creative quality or innovative nature of those plays but rather is a call for Spanish theater to evolve beyond contributions to a canon that has the potential to evoke in public consciousness stereotypes of disempowerment regarding immigrants in Spain.

A Brief History of Spanish Immigration

Prior to the 1980s, Spain had been known as a nation of emigration as millions of Spaniards left the country to escape the dictatorship of Francisco Franco (1939–1975) or to seek better economic opportunities, or both. Many scholars have explored the impact and representation of Spanish emigration in cultural production.[16] Migration in those cases tends to be characterized by nostalgia for a homeland to which it is impossible to return. This romanticization of the homeland does not account for or represent the pain caused by the receptor nation. The national trend of emigration ended in the late 1970s as Spain transitioned to democracy and its economy was on the rise.[17] In 1985, Spain drafted and passed its first immigration law, the *Ley Orgánica sobre los derechos y libertades de los extranjeros en España* (*LO*; Organic Law on the Rights and Liberties of Foreigners in Spain). The law was drafted to facilitate entrance into the European Economic Community, the precursor for the European Union.[18] Its purpose was to regulate the access foreigners had to the Spanish welfare state: education, universal health care, housing, and so forth.

In the preamble of the law was a provision that allowed those with historical connections to Spain (via colonization or exile) to receive preferential treatment in entering Spain:

> Dentro de esta línea merece destacarse la preocupación de la Ley por un tratamiento preferencial en favor de los iberoamericanos, portugueses, filipinos, andorranos, ecuatoguineanos, sefardíes y de los

> originarios de la ciudad de Gibraltar, por darse en ellos los supuestos de identidad o afinidad cultura, que les hacen acreedores a esta consideración.[19]
>
> Within this line of reasoning, the law's concern with preferential treatment toward Ibero-Americans, Portuguese, Filipinos, Andorrans, Equatoguineans, Sephardim, and those from the city of Gibraltar, giving them the assumptions of [Spanish] identity or cultural affinity [with Spain] that make them creditors to this consideration, deserves to be highlighted.

Upon close inspection of this clause, it is worth noting that *moriscos*, that is, Muslims expelled from Spain between the fifteenth and eighteenth centuries, are not included in this list of preferred citizens. Thus, national narratives based on historical antagonisms were woven into this law even before the detailed delineation of foreigners' rights. This provision was removed in the early 1990s after the signing of the Schengen Agreement because nations such as France and Germany had concerns about the volume of people that would have access to all of Europe as a result of the law's provision. Throughout the 1990s and early 2000s, Spain began requiring citizens of the previously preferred nations to apply for a visa to enter the country.

In 1992, six years after joining the EU and in the midst of an economic upswing, Spain hosted four international events that put the nation on the world's stage: Madrid was named the 1992 European Capital of Culture, Barcelona hosted the Summer Olympic Games, Seville hosted the World's Fair (whose theme was "The Age of Discovery"), and Spain celebrated the 500th Anniversary of Christopher Columbus's Arrival to the Americas. Preparation for these four events spawned a construction boom that ushered in the hiring of thousands of migrant workers, mostly from Morocco. The events' economic success caused tourism to grow exponentially, as the notability of Spain's various landscapes (beach, mountainous, urban, rural) became internationally known. In addition, the tourism and general economic booms brought in thousands of agricultural migrant workers to cultivate crops that boosted the nation's international appeal and gastronomic reputation: olives, wine grapes, oranges, and so forth. As a result, agriculture in southern Spain grew so quickly that the proliferation of greenhouses in the area became known as the "Mar de plástico" (Plastic Sea).

The influx of agricultural and construction workers in the early 1990s coincides with the arrival of the first *pateras* and *cayucos* to arrive on the Spanish coasts. *Pateras* are small boats packed with people migrating from Morocco across the Strait of Gibraltar to the coast of mainland Spain, whereas *cayucos* are larger vessels that depart from West African nations such as Mauritania and Senegal, crossing the Atlantic Ocean to reach the Canary Islands. The first regular sightings of *pateras* on the mainland coast were in 1991 and of *cayucos* in the Canary Islands was in 1994.[20] Since then, the *patera* has singlehandedly become the most recognizable image associated with Spanish and European immigration over the past three decades. Within the Spanish context, the *patera* incites memories of the Strait of Gibraltar as the site where the Islamic Empire made landfall in its conquest of the Iberian Peninsula. This historical antagonism, which I detail in chapter 2, is key to understanding the discursive weight of the *patera* as a symbol that precipitates fear and anxiety among the Spanish populace.

The symbolic power of the *patera* has evoked in politicians and the media alike the arousal of autochthonous anxiety and fear of a foreign "invasion." *Patera* crossings account for less than 1 percent of the immigrant population in Spain, however. The discrepancy between the actual data and the general perception is predicated on race as a phobogenic object that is then sensationalized. As Frantz Fanon outlines in *Black Skin, White Masks*, "The Negro is a phobogenic object, provoking anxiety."[21] The stoking of racial fear and anxiety can be traced particularly through the media. As Antonio Bañón Hernández expounds, the media has had a major role in shaping social perceptions on race and immigration in Spain.[22] According to media scholar Teun van Dijk: "The CIPIE data also show that the overall evaluative tendency of the articles [on immigration in the Spanish press] is largely negative: About two-thirds of all articles have topics with negative implications, and only one-sixth of the articles can be classified as rather positive."[23] The repetitive presentation of negative imagery, such as that of the *patera* or dead bodies washing up on Spanish beaches, cements the association of blackness with threats against national security. National anxiety can be better understood upon examination of demographic data. For example, Spain's foreign population in 1998 was a mere 2.9 percent. By 2018, it had grown to 13.3 percent. It is worth noting that "foreign population" refers to anyone in Spain who does not hold Spanish citizenship, because as David Moffette explains:

> Indeed, *extranjero*—foreigner or stranger—is a formal legal category referring to noncitizens present in Spain (international students, tourists, immigrants, and so on), while *inmigrante*—immigrant—is a sociological category referring to those who have left their country and are living in Spain with an intention to stay. While these are legal and somewhat objective distinctions, in common parlance Spaniards often refer to individuals who work in agriculture or in construction as *inmigrantes*, even if they are there temporarily, while white, middle-class immigrants or retired, elderly Europeans living in Spain permanently are often referred to as *extranjeros*, even though they may also be immigrants."[24]

Therefore, over the past twenty years this demographic shift has been construed in racial terms, not only through images of North African and sub-Saharan African immigrants but also through language that distinguishes racialized foreigners from white ones. This distinction exists even though EU and other European citizens migrate to Spain in much larger numbers.

Racial anxiety hit a climactic point in Spain as the immigration rate climbed throughout the early 2000s, because as David Moffette notes, "Between 2000 and 2010, Spain ranked second in the world, behind the United States, as the country with the highest level of annual net immigration."[25] One example of this anxiety is the revisions made to the national immigration law in 2000. The revised law (*Ley Orgánica* 4 [2000]) sharply diminished foreigners' rights, particularly regarding welfare state benefits (education, housing, etc.). The shift in immigration policy reflected national xenophobia that had been exacerbated as the number of immigrants grew exponentially. The March 11, 2004, terrorist attacks in Madrid (known as "11-M") only stoked growing Islamophobia that stemmed from the global war on terrorism.

In 2005, the border fences of Ceuta and Melilla (Spain's two enclaves located on the Moroccan coast) were refortified in response to what Spanish media called the *asalto masivo* (massive assault) that occurred in October of that year, during which, "Hundreds of road-weary Africans descended from their Moroccan forest encampments, threw makeshift ladders onto the border fences circling the territories, and scrambled to climb across . . . Then Moroccan or Spanish security forces—it was never clear who was responsible—fired into the crowds. At least fourteen people died."[26] Originally built between 1995 and 2000, the border fences of Ceuta and Melilla are key loci in Spain's conceptualization of its role as a nation of "Fortress Europe."[27] Parvati Nair eloquently explains how the border fences have created a unique "third space" that is neither Africa nor Europe, making it the only border of its kind in the world.[28] Spain's geopolitical position therefore necessitates constant negotiation of its relationships with Africa and Europe because, as Henk Driessen contends, "since Spain's incorporation into the European Union, its southern border has been transformed into a *European* frontier—a frontier re-marked and reinforced."[29]

Despite more conservative policy and securitization of the border, immigrants continued to flow into Spain until the economic crisis struck the nation in 2008. Southern European nations were drastically hit by the collapse of the global economy, and Spain was no exception. As a result, the number of immigrants entering Spain slowed. The economic crisis provoked anti-immigrant sentiments as Spaniards and immigrants now had to compete for low-wage jobs once disdained by the former. In addition, the extremely high rate of unemployment, particularly for young people (which reached as high as 55 percent), caused many Spanish citizens to emigrate to other EU nations and to the Americas in search of work. In fact, according to data from the Instituto Nacional de Estadística (INE; Spanish Statistical Office), from 2010 to 2015 net migration plummeted below zero as more than a million Spaniards emigrated, coupled with the decline in immigration due to high unemployment.[30] For the first time since the 1990s, the number of immigrants had declined below that of emigrants, and continued to do so for some years. The number of immigrants continued to dip until 2016, when Spain's economy finally began to rebound. Immigration numbers have not reached precrisis levels but now seem to be on a steady climb again as a result of the Syrian Refugee Crisis and the embargo against migrant vessels in Italy, Greece, and Malta. Ending *The Necropolitical Theater* in 2016 serves to bookend an era in Spanish immigration history while also recognizing that the current geopolitical climate of Europe has arisen from anti-immigrant populism.

Methods and the Role of Race

Susanne Zantop notes in her book *Colonial Fantasies*, "It is always curious to note to what extent our critical interests are tied to, or emanate from, our autobiographies."[31] In my case, as a Ghanaian immigrant to the United States (via Spain), immigration has always been a topic of interest and a critical lens through which I examine the world. Even though my immigration story occurred very early in my childhood, it nonetheless constitutes a constant feeling of Otherness and, at times, makes me feel as though homeland is a concept that continuously slips away but that we simultaneously yearn to hold close. In a time when Otherness is under attack by the insidious rise of ethnonationalism, populism, and protectionism, *The Necropolitical Theater* is critical for understanding how Western societies continue to battle against immigration even though racialized immigrant groups (and nonwhite citizens) have for decades declared, "We are here because you were there."[32] In addition, as a black man, race and racial formation have molded my sense of self personally and academically. Similar to homeland, blackness is a sliding concept that varies with space and time. Yet one thing is certain: antiblackness is global, because despite being a social construct, race continues to have tangible effects (knowingly or not) on the lives of billions of people. For this reason, I am acutely aware of how my vantage point as a black man is perceived when conducting and presenting research. It is therefore impossible for me to do literary and cultural analysis without understanding how race plays a role, pun intended. My hope is that *The Necropolitical Theater* provides a framework through which others can make further racial critiques of Spanish cultural works.

The aim of this book is to uncover a racial hierarchy embedded within the genealogy of Spanish immigration plays. Rather than focusing on each immigrant group as an independent entity, analyses of all three immigrant groups will be intertwined through the lens of necropolitics. To achieve this, I spent time in Madrid and Barcelona conducting archival research to gain access to texts and recordings of plays, as well as newspaper reviews. It must be noted that I was unable to see live performances of any of the plays but rather viewed recordings from the archives of the Centro de Documentación Teatral in Madrid and the Teatre Nacional de Catalunya in Barcelona. In addition, I interviewed several playwrights (Ignacio del Moral, David Planell, Jerónimo López Mozo, Irma Correa, Paco Bezerra, and Alberto de Casso) and actors (Mulie Jarju and Armando Buika). These interviews enabled me not only to identify the common rhetorical thread regarding humanization but also to envision the future representation of race and immigration in Spanish theater.

The Necropolitical Theater

The chapters of *The Necropolitical Theater* have been arranged in accordance with the racial hierarchy established in Spanish immigration theater, illustrating the spectrum from necropolitical captivity to physical death and paralleling the degree of blackness of the immigrant group in question. Each chapter intensifies as it descends the hierarchy to demonstrate the gravity of the theatrical patterns of its respective group's representation. Although an argument could be made for a different order, I found that this particular arrangement provided the most dramatic reading of the racial hierarchy that is simultaneously portrayed on and off stage.

Chapter 1, "Are You Being Served? Latin American Female Migrants and Neocolonial Servitude," looks at the gendered migration of Latin Americans, the only immigrant group in which women enter Spain at a higher rate than men.[33] The chapter will explore how this group is marginalized into neocolonial servitude, which I call necropolitical captivity. The captive state is exemplified in the social and professional position in which these women are represented on stage as prostitutes, caretakers, or maids. The relegation to (and representation of) these particular professions is a form of social death as these women are stripped of agency and funneled into servitude, which can be blurred with slavery and domination. The plays I analyze are Alberto de Casso Basterrechea's *Los viernes del Hotel Luna Caribe* (*LVHLC*) (*Fridays at the Caribbean Moon Hotel*) (1997), Luis Araújo's *Mercado libre* (*ML*) (*Free Market*) (2008), and Carmen Resino's *Allegro (ma non troppo)* (*AMNT*) (2008) and *Unos pájaros verdes* (*UPV*) (*Some Green Birds*) (2016). These four plays demonstrate the manner in which Spanish society relies simultaneously on contradictory stereotypes of Latin America women as savage and hypersexual, or as submissive and docile, to denigrate them.[34] These stereotypes empower Spanish male characters to prey on vulnerable women, and in some cases, trap them in lives of gendered servitude. These plays, which take place in gendered spaces such as brothels, kitchens, and bedrooms, further highlight the ways the social death of this group is enforced by Spanish masculinity, machismo, and vestiges of colonial power. Finally, in some of the plays examined, there is a desire and/or an ability to return to the homeland.

That these women can return to the homeland is tied to the colonial and contemporary political connections between Spain and Latin American nations because unlike the other groups discussed in this book, they are able to enter and leave Spain legally. Latin American immigrants present an Other whose tongue and culture are rooted in Spain, which facilitates superficial ease of interaction compared with African migrants (notwithstanding prejudices based on physical features).

Chapter 2, "The Second Reconquista: Maurophobia and the Impossibility of North African Migrants in Spain," examines how popular, contemporary interpretations of Reconquista (711–1492) rhetoric are being recycled and reinvigorated against present-day Moroccan and North African migrants, thus establishing a Second Reconquista grounded in what Ricard Zapata-Barrero calls "Maurophobia" (fear of the Moors).[35] Rather than the previous racialized dynamic of Christians versus Muslims, the present perceived battle is between the West and the Islamic world, which is seen as unable to adapt to the "progressive" lifestyle found in Western nations such as Spain. This dynamic, which Etienne Balibar coined as "racism without races," leaves only two options for North African/Middle Eastern migrants: assimilate or face social marginalization due to autochthonous anxieties regarding terrorism. This chapter illustrates how plays reveal a new version of the Reconquista now framed in terms of culture as incompatible, undesirable, and suspicious. The plays analyzed are *Ahlán* by Jerónimo López Mozo (1997), *Bazar* by David Planell (1997), and *Ataque preventivo (AP)* (*Preventive Attack*) by Juan Pablo Heras (2005). In each of these plays, regardless of the amount of time that they have been living in Spain and despite attempts to integrate into Spanish society, the North African characters are constantly reminded and made aware of their Otherness. This social barrier results in the need to erase parts of their identity—whether that is their mother language, religion, or sexuality—as a way of obtaining Spanishness. The erasure (or ontological death) fails to achieve Spanishness, however, developing a narrative in which integration is ultimately impossible.

Chapter 3, "En Route to Death: Spanish Necropolitical Theater and the Precarity of Black Immigration," analyzes how the Spanish stage creates an environment that consistently facilitates the death of black male migrants. Their inability to survive the play connotes a morbid message about Spain's relation to blackness, which is consumed for the sake of provoking emotional responses regarding the humanity of blackness and simultaneously rejected out of fear. These narrative tropes of black bodies as phobogenic objects and black death constitute the final and most brutal piece of the racial hierarchy. Black characters are not only depicted as inferior but also as undeserving of living in Spain, if at all. The plays I will analyze in this chapter are *La mirada del hombre oscuro* by Ignacio del Moral (1991), which is the first play to explicitly portray the Spanish immigration question; *La falsa muerte de Jaro el Negro* (*The False Death of Jaro the Negro*) by Fernando Martín Iniesta

(1997); and *Friday* by Irma Correa (2011). These three works encapsulate the degree to which the physical death of the sub-Saharan African migrant is used as a didactical instrument for the spectator by highlighting not only the precarity of the border—land, sea, air—that these migrants cross, but also that of their bodies as phobogenic agents of Otherness inhabiting the Spanish national stage in both literal and figurative terms.

The book's conclusion, "The Necropolitical Theater of Whiteness," reaffirms that studying the exclusion, isolation, and/or subjugation of racialized immigrant groups in theatrical representations provides a greater understanding of Spain's conceptualization of the immigration experience. The racial patterns developed on stage reflect the workings of Spain's racial hierarchy. In uncovering the hierarchy, *The Necropolitical Theater* illustrates how Spanish immigration plays form a necropolitical theater of whiteness that is advanced via national dramaturgy prizes, which award plays that ostensibly humanize immigrants but actually use them as simple plot devices to reflect racial anxieties. All the plays, though focused on immigrants, are also making major statements on whiteness as they teach how one should perform whiteness. In the conclusion, I present an alternative to necropolitical theater known as the *convivial theater*, derived from the Spanish word *convivencia*, which means to live together. Such a theatrical approach would require playwrights to create plays that better reflect the realities of immigrants without relying on sensationalizing tropes that promote hegemonic whiteness and mere survivability for nonwhites. Only by embracing the notion of the convivial theater will Spanish theater hold itself accountable to the multicultural and multiracial (present and) future of Spain.

Chapter 1

Are You Being Served?

Latin American Female Migrants and Neocolonial Servitude

Spain's connection with Latin America is often conceptualized as a transatlantic familial bond created by the historical legacy of colonization, which now manifests itself via cultural markers such as language and religion. This bond is evident in the common reference to Spain as *La Madre Patria* (the Motherland). As discussed in the introduction, this bond was recognized and embedded into immigration policy in 1985 with the creation of the *Ley Orgánica sobre los derechos y libertades de los extranjeros en España* (*LO*). While the preferential treatment bestowed to those who have been directly affected by Spain's colonial past is a benevolent postcolonial gesture, Spain's entrance into the European Union rendered this ephemeral.[1] Upon the implementation of the Schengen Agreement in 1995, Spain began to remove such language from its immigration policy to prevent the possibility of migrants freely flowing into other European nations. The supranational mandate of the Schengen Zone is the catalyst for Spain's transformation into a guardian of "Fortress Europe," the nations whose responsibility it is to block migration to Europe (e.g., Spain, Italy, Greece, and Portugal).

Throughout the 1990s, Spain increased restrictions and required visas for individuals from nations that previously were allowed to enter freely. As Ruben Andersson notes, "It is no coincidence that the first reported arrivals of *pateras*, or migrant boats, around the Strait of Gibraltar occurred in 1991, the year when Spain joined the Schengen Agreement for free movement within the European Union and introduced visa requirements for Moroccans."[2] Furthermore, David Moffette points out that despite "plans to reinstate visa requirements for Algerians, Moroccans and Tunisians, soon to join the nationals of another 113 countries on the tourist visa list, [Spain maintained] the visa exemption for Ibero-Americans."[3] However, this too was short lived: Dominicans and Peruvians were added to the list in 1995, as Spain ratified the Schengen Agreement.[4] This came to a head in 2001, when Colombia was added to the list of nations from which a visa would be required to enter

Spain. On March 18, 2001, Nobel Prize–winning novelist Gabriel García Márquez penned a letter in response to the decision, stating that he would not return to Spain until the decision was reversed. The letter, cosigned by more than 150 Colombian artists and intellectuals, decried the decision as a political slap in the face because "La solidaridad cultural de las naciones hispanas y americanas, no puede ser simplemente un asunto retórico" (The cultural solidarity of Hispanic and American nations cannot be a mere rhetorical matter).[5] Citing the historical ties between Colombia and Spain, García Márquez forcefully states, "Explíquenles a sus socios europeos que ustedes tienen con nosotros una obligación y un compromiso históricos a los que no pueden dar la espalda" (Explain to your European partners that you have a historical obligation to and agreement with us that you cannot turn your back on).[6] This quotation gets to the core of the quandary: Spain was forced to choose between reconciling with its colonial past or maintaining its membership in the in-group that is the European Union. Spain chose to side with its European counterparts, but in making that choice, created the conditions under which the undocumented migration of Latin Americans could proliferate since, as an unintended consequence of the visa decision, many Latin Americans came legally with a visa, but then overstayed their visa, leaving them undocumented within Spain.

This historical context helps to explain the findings of a United Nations report stating that between 1999 and 2006, the Latin American population in Spain had multiplied sixfold.[7] The report also highlights that Latin American migrants are the best valued in Spanish society since their capacity to integrate due to shared cultural markers and values makes them a more desirable migrant group (3). Although Spain did not lift the visa requirement, Latin Americans have a much faster path to Spanish residency and citizenship than other nationalities (two years versus up to ten years). Despite their large numbers over the years, Latin Americans are not particularly regarded as "invading" Spain as African migrants are because (1) they most often enter legally (with a visa); (2) colonial history provides a context for them being in Spain (i.e., "We are here because you were there"); and (3) Latin American migration is predominately female, connoting a less threatening influx than that of other groups. To avoid falling into a binary of "acceptable" and "unacceptable" immigrants, the preference for Latin American over other non-European immigrants must be understood as part of Spain's intention to create a nation in which *hispanidad* (Hispanic identity) is privileged. As Enakshi Dua explains in the context of Canadian nation building, "producing a racialized nation can take place not only through practices of exclusion, but also through practices of inclusion."[8] Therefore, the preferential inclusion of Latin American migrants enables the unwritten, yet desired, exclusion of other groups.

In relation to other migrant groups, only Latin American immigration has a higher percentage of women than men entering the country, with approximately 54 percent women to 46 percent men. Furthermore, this discrepancy is considerable when looking at specific nations, particularly those in the Caribbean and Andean regions. The feminization of the Latin American migratory flow creates a peculiar gendered dynamic that manifests itself in the social and professional lives of these women. It is here that I would like to make an intervention regarding the necropolitics of Latin American migration. This group, though heavily racialized, has high levels of acceptance among the Spanish populace because, as Antonio Izquierdo Escribano and Raquel Martínez-Buján propound, "The internal job market values the linguistic identity of Latin American workers, as it makes communication with these workers easier, be it to perform their duties in home and care services or in the restaurant, hotel and café industries."[9] Latin American women, particularly Afro-Caribbean women, are often relegated to roles of servitude: caretakers, maids, nannies, and prostitutes. This gendered professionalization forms a zombie state in which these women are physically alive but socially dead as a result of their status. Their necropolitical status in Spain is portrayed in several plays, most notably Alberto de Casso Basterrechea's *Los viernes del Hotel Luna Caribe* (*LVHLC*) (1997), Luis Araújo's *Mercado libre* (*ML*) (2008), and Carmen Resino's *Allegro (ma non troppo)* (*AMNT*) (2008) and *Unos pájaros verdes* (*UPV*) (2016). These four plays illustrate the manner in which servitude via prostitution or domestic service creates a gendered power dynamic that renders the Latin American women trapped within the confines of the private sphere: the brothel or the home. This dynamic is further complicated by the fact that these women are typically Afro-Caribbean, hailing from Cuba and the Dominican Republic, which implicates stereotypes of the sexuality of black womanhood that date back to slavery. Finally, though men and women often migrate for the betterment of themselves or their families, the migration of women in Spanish literature is not presented as an adventure but rather as a cautionary tale. Although female migrants do not usually die in their respective stories, the didactic message at the end tends to be that they would have been better off if they had not migrated at all. Migration thus functions as a counterproductive venture. In propagating a pattern in which female migrants are unsuccessful in attaining access to Spanish society, they are relegated to a necropolitical zombie status, neither dead nor alive, but always at your service.

The Chains of Prostitution in *Los viernes del Hotel Luna Caribe and Mercado libre*

Alberto de Casso Basterrechea's 1997 play *Los viernes del Hotel Luna Caribe* highlights how migrants are lured to Spain by false hope and false job contracts, thereby ensnaring them as unauthorized migrants. Once trapped, these migrants find themselves between the rock of the state and the hard place of the institutions and people that have trapped them. The play is the story of a Cuban family—Régula Laínez and her two daughters, Liena and Yliana—that receives contracts to come from Havana to work at Orlando Domínguez's Hotel Luna Caribe, located outside Madrid. Act 1 takes place on the day that the three women arrive at the hotel. Upon arriving, they realize that it is not a hotel at all but rather a roadside brothel. Régula and Liena reject Orlando's work offer and leave in a taxi for Madrid. Yliana, however, decides to stay, becoming the *reina de las putas* (queen of the prostitutes).[10] Act 2, which takes place three months later, immerses the spectator in the wild nightlife of the Hotel Luna Caribe. By deciding to stay, Yliana becomes Orlando's most prized possession: the prostitute everyone wants but no one can have. She is gradually enthralled by Miguel San Juan, a young police officer who often visits Hotel Luna Caribe as a client. It turns out that he lives next door to Liena and Régula in Alcalà de Henares (a nearby suburb), and thus begins to pass messages between the sisters. He offers to help Yliana escape from the concrete prison that is the Hotel Luna Caribe, but she declines. Months later, Liena comes to visit and to give her sister a birthday gift, a blue dress covered in butterflies. They are able to bond and catch up in private. Liena asks her sister if she wants to escape this life, but Yliana has resigned herself to her captor and the conditions in which she lives. When Liena leaves, Orlando returns with a massive birthday gift for Yliana: a cage with a Siamese cat inside. Almost immediately after she opens the gift, policemen show up to accuse Orlando of running a prostitution ring. As the police arrest Orlando, Yliana asks Miguel for ten thousand pesetas, which she puts in Orlando's pocket as a parting gift. She then seduces Miguel to take off his clothes. In that compromising moment, Liena returns to see her sister with her fiancé. Having destroyed everyone's emotional links to her, Yliana walks out of the hotel and is hit by a tractor trailer. The play's third act, entitled "act 0," is a flashback to the Laínez family's life in Havana before they left for Madrid. This act, though presented as the past, contains elements of the previous two acts, which helps the spectator to close the narrative circle.

Unlike her sister and mother, Yliana is very much aware of the reality of the Hotel Luna Caribe. This is in part because in Cuba she used her experience in the hospitality industry to court foreign men on the Havana pier. As their neighbor Jessica quips, "Al menos yo no tengo que ir a pasearme al malecón a partir de las diez de la noche para poder comprarme una trusa" (At least I don't have to walk around the pier starting at 10 P.M. to be able to buy panties) (*LVHLC*, 110). When Yliana quips back with an insult, Omar (Jessica's father) intervenes and slaps her, saying, "A mi hija no le hablas así, jinetera . . . de mierda . . . jinetera gusana de mierda. ¿Entendido? Si no fuera por tu madre te rompía la boca" (Don't speak that way to my daughter, slut . . . fucking refugee slut. Got it? If it weren't for your mother, I'd smash your mouth in) (*LVHLC*, 110). Key to Omar's violent response is the use of the words *jinetera* and *gusana*. The first, *jinetera*, refers to a Cuban woman who engages in illegal business with foreigners, particularly prostitution. On the other hand, *gusana* refers to a Cuban woman opposed to the postrevolution government (i.e., the Castro regime), who therefore leaves the country. The pejorative remarks come as no surprise to spectators, as Yliana's life as a prostitute in Spain has already been observed.

Yliana's role as a prostitute exemplifies what I call necropolitical captivity, a state in which the captive is never killed but rather socially and mentally dead to the rest of society through isolation and marginalization. It is in this state that so many Latin American female migrants are portrayed on stage. Within this framework, we can better understand Yliana's ability to survive in the Hotel Luna Caribe and why she dies upon leaving the hotel for the first time since having entered. Necropolitical captivity is most clearly demonstrated in act 2 when Orlando goes to extreme measures to make Yliana happy staying at the hotel, when Miguel San Juan and Liena on two separate occasions ask Yliana if she wishes to escape the confines of the hotel, and by the symbolic birthday gift that Orlando buys her. These three scenes illustrate Yliana's desire for change but inability to act on it until the end.

Act 2 begins with a typical Friday night party at the Hotel Luna Caribe, packed with clients drinking at the bar and engaging with the prostitutes in the curtained-off zones. At the end of the night, Orlando notices that Yliana has spent almost the entire night talking to the same client, Cliente Joven (Young Client), who happens to be the police officer who appears at the end of act 1. Orlando takes her onto the dance floor to dance and expresses his desire for her:

ORLANDO DOMÍNGUEZ. Cuando te mira parece hipnotizado . . . como si sólo te viera a ti.
YLIANA. Aquí no se ve nada ni a nadie con tanta oscuridad . . . ni siquiera se ven las estrellas desde la ventana de mi cuarto con las farolas de la autopista.
ORLANDO DOMÍNGUEZ. Sí tú me lo pides las haré fundir con mi escopeta para que esta noche veas las estrellas . . . aunque luego se despeñen tres camiones o venga tu poli a ponerme una multa.
. . .
YLIANA. Sí, harías tantas cosas . . . que ni siquiera . . . me dejas salir a tomar el aire a tres metros del Hotel.
ORLANDO DOMÍNGUEZ. Nunca me lo has pedido.
YLIANA. Esas cosas no hay que pedirlas, se dan por hecho. Me tienes aquí enclaustrada como una monja. (92)

ORLANDO DOMÍNGUEZ. When he looks at you he's hypnotized . . . as if he only sees you.
YLIANA. You can't see anything or anyone in all this darkness . . . you can't even see the stars from the window in my room with all the lights on the highway.

ORLANDO DOMÍNGUEZ. If you ask me, I'll blow them out with my shotgun so that you see the stars tonight . . . even though later three trucks will veer off the road or your officer will come and fine me.

. . .

YLIANA. Yeah, you would do many things . . . but you won't even . . . let me step outside three meters from the hotel to breathe fresh air.

ORLANDO DOMÍNGUEZ. You've never asked me.

YLIANA. You shouldn't have to ask for such things; they should be a given. You have me cloistered here like a nun.

This excerpt demonstrates that Yliana has not stepped outside of the hotel for three months (the end of act 1), engendering a sense of frustration in response to a lack of agency that she feels should be a human right. This deprivation of agency is compared to the experience of a nun, which is ironic because nuns choose a cloistered life as an expression of their faith and devotion. In addition, within the confines of the nunnery, nuns have much more agency regarding the quotidian matters of their lives than Yliana does. Yliana, however, is cloistered as the result of fear because at this point in the play, she has learned nothing of her mother and sister, and thus has nowhere else to go if she were to leave. This reference underscores the way prostitutes and nuns can be seen as experiencing flip sides of the same coin, as both are cloistered and controlled in confined spaces to serve the patriarchal will.

This is not the only instance in which Yliana compares herself to a religious figure. Later in act 2 when Liena comes to visit Yliana on her birthday, Orlando gives the sisters some time to talk in private. During this time, Liena tries to find out how her sister is able to withstand life as a prostitute:

LIENA. ¿Cómo puedes soportar este tipo de vida?

YLIANA. Le tengo que echar mucho "amor propio" . . .

LIENA. ¿Qué dices?

YLIANA. Lo que oyes . . . tengo que echarle mucho "amor propio" a la cosa.

(*Ríen divertidas.*)

LIENA. ¿Y eso?

YLIANA. Me tiene como a la Virgen del Cobre, tras de un vitral. Al final, me va a poner en un hueco rodeada de cirios y va a llamar al Papa para que me canonicen. (99)

LIENA. How can you put up with this type of life?

YLIANA. I have to add a lot of "self-love" . . .

LIENA. What are you saying?

YLIANA. What you heard . . . I have to add a lot of "self-love" to things.

(*They laugh, amused.*)

LIENA. Why?

YLIANA. He has me like the Virgin of El Cobre, behind a stained-glass window. In the end, he will put me in a space surrounded by altar candles and he'll call the pope so they canonize me.

This comical exchange between the two sisters reveals two important pieces of Yliana's life in the Hotel Luna Caribe: First, she is not being taken advantage of sexually nor engaging in any sexual activity with Orlando or any clients. Rather, she pleasures herself sexually to endure the solitude in the sex-as-work environment. Second, Orlando parades her around as his pride and joy, an unattainable standard for all, himself included. In a similar fashion, the Virgin of El Cobre, the Patroness of Cuba, is the pinnacle of Catholic icons in Cuba, an unattainable standard of womanhood, motherhood, faith, and devotion. This unlikely comparison between a chaste prostitute and the Virgin Mary is comical for the two sisters and spectators because each case presents the impossible as possible. This exchange therefore furthers the argument made earlier about nuns and prostitutes, as neither Yliana nor the Virgin Mary is allowed agency in their roles as chaste figures because both function as objects of male fervor, whether spiritual or carnal.

Yliana's ability to make light of her situation gives the initial impression that she is doing well, but when probed further by her sister, she reveals the truth behind her sequestered life:

> Entonces . . . es que yo nunca le he pedido permiso para ir a ningún lado. No es que me hayan faltado ganas y oportunidades . . . pero es que . . . al principio . . . no se lo pedía por orgullo . . . y al final . . . sabes, me he acostumbrado . . . como una leona loca supongo que se acostumbra a su jaula . . . a estar en mi cuarto todo el día . . . reflejada en todos los espejos . . . a veces me pregunto . . . cómo no se aburren de reflejarme . . . Es que me entra como un manojo de nervios . . . acercarme a esa autopista . . . y alejarme más de tres metros de aquí. Pasan tantos camiones. Una noche me dediqué a contarlos. Pasaron más de mil. (*LVHLC*, 100)

> Well . . . it's that I have never asked him for permission to go anywhere. It's not that I've not wanted to; it's that at the beginning, I didn't ask him out of pride . . . and in the end, you know, I've gotten used to it . . . I guess like a wild lioness gets used to her cage. To be in my room all day, reflected in all the mirrors, sometimes I ask myself, "How do they not get bored of reflecting me?" It's that I turn into a nervous wreck getting near the highway and going further than three meters from here. So many trucks pass by. One night, I focused on counting them. More than a thousand passed by.

By comparing herself to a lioness who grows accustomed to life in a cage, Yliana demonstrates necropolitical captivity: although she is not dead, her life is void of meaning and substance as she is a social pariah and has lost hope of escape or change. This loss of self is made evident in her reflection (pun intended) on mirrors. Spending most of her day in a room full of mirrors, she is reflected and multiplied as object rather than as subject, as demonstrated by the grammar of "cómo no se aburren de reflejarme." The multitude of mirrors in the room thus refract and obfuscate her subjectivity such that she gradually submits to the conditions of her captivity. Yliana's phobia of the highway and the speeding trucks that routinely pass by the hotel is not only a result of the trauma caused by Maria La Portuguesa's death in act 1 but also a foreshadowing of her own death in act 2 when she finally does leave the hotel.

The existential loss that Yliana expresses to her sister is symbolically cemented in the gift that Orlando gives her after Liena leaves: an expensive Siamese cat in a cage. As Orlando explains, "Es una gata siamesa . . . tan hermosa y tan independiente como tú . . . por eso pensé que os llevaríais bien" (It's a Siamese cat . . . so pretty and independent like you . . . that's why I thought you two would get along well) (*LVHLC*, 101–2). What he does not tell her is that the cat is worth "cien noches de amor de cada una de mis putas" (one hundred nights of sex from each of his prostitutes), implying that Yliana is worth more than all the other prostitutes combined, for the reasons discussed earlier (*LVHLC*, 102). The juxtaposition that Orlando makes between the beauty and temperament of the cat and that of Yliana serves as a symbolic representation of the latter's elevated status within the Hotel Luna Caribe. Yliana is worth more than all the others not because of the economic value of her sexual labor, as she has been chaste for months, but rather because of the intangible romantic potential that Orlando sees in her. Furthermore, the presentation of the Siamese cat in a cage reflects Yliana's position as a woman who is simultaneously sexually objectified and paraded for other men to see, yet never touch.

As Yliana's value is grounded in her unattainability, her desire to leave the hotel is her ultimate downfall. Her death at the end of act 2 is reminiscent of the death of Maria La Portuguesa in act 1, who is killed by a truck that miscalculates the curve just before the hotel and ends up striking her. Wearing the new blue butterfly dress that Liena gave her as a birthday gift, Yliana walks out triumphantly, announcing that she is returning to Cuba with her mother, who was in a car accident some months prior and is very unhappy in Spain. Her seemingly victorious exit ends abruptly because, as the stage directions note: "*Yliana sale. Nadie se mira, como si todos se hubieran quedado solos, aturdidos por el dolor, para siempre. Unos instantes más tarde se oye el chirrido de un camión aterradoramente próximo derrapar en la autopista. Oscuro. La luna del espejo se destriza en mil pedazos*" (Yliana leaves. No one looks at each other; it is as if all of them have been left alone, stunned by the pain, forever. Some moments later, the screech of a skidding truck is heard frighteningly close on the highway. Blackout. The moon mirror shatters into a thousand pieces) (*LVHLC*, 104). Yliana's exit and subsequent death stun the other characters present because she disrupts everyone's narrative path. Orlando has been arrested for running a prostitution ring and no longer has his "Virgin de El Cobre," as Yliana gives him ten thousand pesetas to make him think that she had sex with Miguel San Juan. Miguel's marriage to Liena may no longer happen as she catches him with Yliana in one of the private beds, both topless. This self-destructive scene is the path to liberation for Yliana: breaking affective links with everyone except her mother (who is not present in the scene), Yliana is able to leave the Hotel Luna Caribe, only to walk into her own death.

Yliana's and Maria La Portuguesa's deaths are mirrored at the end of act 0 when a car skids off the road a block from their house in Havana, killing one woman. The car almost kills Liena, who, having thrown herself to the ground, is spared as the car flies over her. The other woman who is standing next to her, however, is struck and killed instantly. Liena describes the death of this woman: "Su cara era un . . . amasijo de sangre. Tenía un ojo salido de su órbita . . . en el pecho . . . como si fuera un broche" (Her face was a . . . blob of blood. One of her eyes had popped out of its socket . . . on her chest . . . as if it were a brooch) (*LVHLC*, 113). This eye continues to haunt Liena in Madrid as she works in a sausage factory, confronted daily with the bloody masses of pork that she sorts through, sometimes imagining an eye looking up at her. We have no description of Yliana's physical state after the crash, as act 2 ends in that moment, but it is not far-fetched to speculate that her body is mangled similarly to that of the woman killed in Havana, especially since both women wear the same blue dress covered in butterflies.

The repetition and refraction of these deaths in each act evokes the mirror imagery in Yliana's room, where she is an object reflected and infinitely contained in the repetition of the mirrors, which represents her objectification by patriarchal power. The focus on death at the end of acts 2 and 0 beckons back to the first words in the text, the epigraph, "La muerte es la mejor de las desgracias porque borra todas las demás" (Death is the best of all misfortunes, for it erases all the others).[11] This quote comes from Cuban poet Nancy Morejón's poem entitled "Tata a la muerte de Don Pablo" (Tata at the Death of Don Pablo). In the case of Yliana, it seems that Tata is right: death was the path to liberation. I do not interpret Yliana's death as a suicide, as her last line, "Regreso a Cuba . . . con mi madre" (I'm returning to Cuba . . . with my mother), establishes intentionality (*LVHLC*, 104). Rather, her courage to step out of the Hotel Luna Caribe is an act of freedom that is symbolically annihilated by the truck that hits her. Yliana's decision to return to Cuba is a rejection of the patriarchal and chauvinistic space of the brothel, demonstrated by the fact that she is returning to care for her ailing mother. For that reason, she must leave the space if she is ever to achieve agency. Her inability to move freely is entrapping her more than the space itself. As philosopher Neil Roberts beautifully puts it, *marronage* is "a total refusal of the enslaved condition."[12] The act of fleeing rather than the future destination is what facilitates Yliana's feeling of freedom. It is thus fitting that once she has achieved personal freedom, her story line would end tragically, because it is her misfortune that drives the plot. Unlike the *cimarrones* (runaway slaves, or "maroons"), from which the term *marronage* is derived, Yliana seeks refuge in the colonized space, the city of Havana, because it provides familiarity, social interaction, and the possibility of employment via her entrepreneurship. In addition, the brothel not only represents the sexual objectification and servitude of women but given its location on the highway and the large quantity of trucks that pass by, it also represents commerce. It is, quite literally, sex traffic that kills her, thereby creating a message about the commodification of sex within the global economy, rooted in the objectification of women.

Act 0's function as a flashback didactically demonstrates that the migration of the Laínez family was doomed from the start. This predetermination, manifested in the narrative return to the point of origin, is a trope that appears to be common as far as female migrants are concerned. The moral of the story suggests that the women would have been better off staying at the place of origin, and as such, the migration has been in vain. This fatalistic trope engenders pity but detracts from the true problem underlying the stories: the terrible people (usually men) who made their migration fatal. The anachronism of act 0 as the final act mirrors the failure of colonial return, wherein the formerly colonized return to the metropole to colonize it. Rather than colonize Spain, however, the Laínez women are lured, entrapped, and colonized by Spanish men, cementing their journey's fatalism.

As part of the necropolitical turn in Spanish theater, this fatalism is found in other plays, including Luis Araújo's 2008 *Mercado libre* (*ML*; *Free Market*). This two-person play is the story of A (described in the stage directions as *ciudadano* [a male citizen]) and B (described as *indocumentada* [undocumented woman]).[13] The lack of proper names allows for universality and promotes the translatability of the work. B is a prostitute who works for A. Over time, the relationship becomes more and more physically abusive, until B decides to leave. When her two adolescent sons are at risk of being jailed and deported for allegedly raping a female classmate, B desperately turns to A, because he is a corporate lawyer. The price for his help is that she becomes his property, with whom he can do whatever he wants. The plays ends with A explaining to some people at what may be a press conference that B has disappeared and that he has therefore taken custody of her three children and has begun the paperwork for them to receive citizenship while the authorities search for her.

The gradual and severe degradation of B's psyche and humanity throughout the play not only highlights violence against women but also the inability of the state to protect society's most vulnerable people. Luis Foronda (a member of the jury that selected *Mercado libre* for the X Esperpento Competition for

Theatrical Texts) notes that B "es una mujer envuelta en un mundo de fatalidades alimentadas por la necesidad y por el miedo, haciendo bueno el dicho que cualquiera puede dominar un sufrimiento, excepto el que lo padece. Aparentar ser ciudadanos respetables o vivir sin documentos ni futuro son las dos únicas maneras de estar en el mundo que nos quedan" (is a woman mixed up in a world of misfortunes nurtured by necessity and fear, fulfilling the saying that everyone can master a grief but he that has it. To feign to be respectable citizens or live without documents or a future are the only two ways to be in this world we live in).[14] The binary that Foronda proposes implies that all citizens are complicit in the treatment of undocumented people. No matter how respectable we may appear, we are contributing (directly or indirectly) to a vicious underworld that lives off the necessity of these migrants to provide a life for themselves and their families and off the fear that they have of being deported. It is necessity and fear that drive B to the extreme measures she takes to ensure a better life for her children.

At the core of this play is a critique of how society's obsession with attributing economic value to all things exacerbates inequality and privilege, thereby creating situations in which the morally bankrupt can prevail if they have enough money. As Antonio Daniel García Orellana (the previous year's winner of the X Esperpento competition and a jury member) points out in his prologue to the text: "Araújo pone en entredicho la existencia de una sociedad justa, igualitaria. Señala la desigualdad de oportunidades en una sociedad que alardea de oportunidades iguales para sus ciudadanos" (Araújo calls into question the existence of a just, egalitarian society. He points out that inequality of opportunities in a society that boasts about equal opportunity for all its citizens).[15] While this is true, his statement leaves out people like B, who are undocumented and therefore are not afforded access to those opportunities by default. The inequality of citizenship, exacerbated by the patriarchal, transactional dynamic of prostitution, creates a dangerous environment for B from the start. A is a metaphorical representation of the state who comes to symbolize the process of forced assimilation. Throughout the play, his objective to make B his personal possession is rooted in her lack of state protection as an undocumented immigrant. Her desire to grant her three children a better life via assimilation and citizenship is achieved at the expense of herself, physically and mentally. Her erasure in scene 15, the play's final scene, demonstrates that the price of citizenship is a complete silencing (she is gagged at the end of scene 14) for the sake of her children. Similarly, with forced assimilation, the immigrant's culture is silenced, and by doing so, the children are assimilated into the receptor culture.

Mercado libre is composed of "quince escenas que muestran lo que la sociedad no quiere ver, una realidad hipócrita y perversa, donde lo inhumano se hace natural (más dolor)" (fifteen scenes that show what society does not what to see, a hypocritical and perverse reality, where the inhumane becomes natural [plus pain]).[16] This reality is foreshadowed in scene 1 when

B says goodbye to A after a sexual encounter, to which he responds, "Hasta mañana . . . prenda" (See you tomorrow . . . darling!) (*ML*, 19). Although the word *prenda* can signify a term of endearment, the use of the ellipsis indicates that the word is a double entendre referring to its standard meanings: a garment, a gift, or a token; all of these underscore the objectification of B. His farewell marks the beginning of an increasingly possessive dynamic, which is made more apparent in scene 2 when he says: "Quiero que seas mía. Sentir que me perteneces" (I want you to be mine—feel that you belong to me) (*ML*, 19). José Monleón explains: "El poder paga. Y paga más, simplemente, para conseguir más" (Power pays. And it pays more simply to get more).[17] A is insatiable, and at times inconsolable, until he ultimately gets what he wants.

A perfect example of this desire occurs during scenes 4 through 5 when A states that he wants to rape B, an idea to which she is at first vehemently opposed, but to which she later acquiesces under the condition of receiving one month's pay. Scene 6 begins with the following stage direction: "*B tiene la cara marcada. Algún cardenal o raspón en brazos y piernas*" (There is a mark on B's face. [And] some bruises or scrapes on her arms and legs) (*ML*, 39). These bodily marks are the result of the brutal ambush, as A dragged her down the sidewalk, beat her, and raped her. Outraged because she will not be able to work for two months while her body heals, B demands double the money. This leads to a debate on the value of sex:

A. Todo tiene su precio, ¿no te acuerdas?
B. ¡Todo no!
A. ¡Ya lo creo que sí!
B. Esto no, hijo de puta, esto no tiene precio.
A. Se lo pusiste tú.
B. Pero no era por esto.
A. Tú misma dices que eso vale el doble.
B. ¡Pues dámelo!
A. ¿Lo ves? Ése es el precio. (*ML*, 41)

A. Everything has a price. Don't you remember?
B. Not everything!
A. I think so!
B. This doesn't, son of a bitch! This doesn't have a price.
A. You set the price.
B. But it wasn't for this.
A. You yourself just said it's worth double.
B. Then give it to me!
A. See? That is the price.

A's shrewd knowledge of corporate transactions allows him to logically outsmart B, such that she agrees to and puts the price on her own rape. This manipulation is then used to justify his abuse. He ultimately gives her the money, but the transactional nature of their relationship brings him closer to his goal of possessing B as a sexual object.

Acquiescing to A's sexual perversity to help her children, B has become a different woman—no longer just a prostitute but rather an indentured, sexual servant with whom A can conduct painful practices. In scene 8, B delivers a heart-wrenching monologue regarding the price she has paid to obtain freedom for her children:

> Tendrán una vida, una vida de verdad. Yo no la he tenido, pero se la daré a ellos. Sigue deseándome, úsame . . . abusa de mí y podré darles una vida. Les pagaré unos estudios, aprenderán un oficio. Quién sabe. La niña es bien inteligente . . . Puede que hasta vaya a la universidad. Los mayores ya no, ya conocen la angustia. Pero trabajarán, son resistentes.
>
> Me preguntas qué pienso cuando me lastimas. Eso pienso: les estoy comprando una vida. No como la de su madre. No como la tuya. A ti nadie te querrá nunca. Una vida de verdad.
>
> Nadie ha notado nada. No se me ven las marcas. Nadie sabe. Me duele al caminar, me roza la ropa. Pero nadie ve nada. Sentada en la cafetería de Cuzco, a través de mis gafas del sol, observo a las users españolas. Llevan bolsas de tiendas elegantes. Yo ahora también, a veces. Soy una más. Casi no se me nota ya el acento. He pagado mi precio, ya no siento la culpa. El dolor la ha matado. Ya no veo miradas recelosas. He comprado por fin la indiferencia. Una mujer anónima con un vermú con soda y unas gafas de sol. El puto paraíso de la Europa rica. Cómo desprecio el perdón que me vendéis, la indiferencia . . . ¡La libertad era esto! (*ML*, 53)

> They will have a life, a real life. I haven't had this, but I will give it to them. Keep desiring me. Use me . . . abuse me and I'll be able to give them a life. I'll pay for their studies, they will learn a trade. Who knows. The little girl is so smart . . . She could maybe even go to university. The older boys can't; they already have angst. But they will work, they're tough.
>
> You ask me what I think when you hurt me. This is what I think: I'm buying them a life. Not like the one their mother has. Not like yours. No one will ever love you. A real life.
>
> No one has noticed anything. My bruises aren't visible. No one knows. It hurts to walk, clothing chafes my skin. But no one sees anything. Seated in the Cuzco cafeteria, through my sunglasses I observe the Spanish women. They carry purses from fancy stores. Now I do, too, sometimes. I'm just another woman. You can barely note my accent now. I've paid my price; I don't feel guilty anymore. The pain

> has killed the guilt. I don't see the suspicious looks anymore. I've finally bought indifference. An anonymous woman with a vermouth and soda, and sunglasses. The fucking paradise of rich Europe. How I despise the forgiveness that you sell me, the indifference . . . This was freedom!

Notable here is B's resignation to the pain and abuse, similar to Yliana's in *Los viernes del Hotel Luna Caribe*. In B's case, however, there is a clearly stated objective: obtaining a better life for her three kids. In addition to the physical pain, B also erases her identity: her accent, her style of dress, and so forth. By becoming more like the posh, Spanish women she sees in Cuzco (an upper-class area of Madrid), B is consequently being beat into anonymity that could, and later does, result in her disappearance.

B's freedom is predicated on two things: the outside world not seeing the physical effects of abuse and her ability to be perceived as just another Spanish woman. What we observe in the monologue is freedom *from* poverty and perceived Otherness (i.e., Isaiah Berlin's concept of negative liberty). If indifference can lead to freedom, it is because indifference connotes the inability to perceive barriers to your freedom. Indifference obscures her difference. Sadly, B views her relationship to A through a transactional lens, which obfuscates her ability to understand his nefarious goal of possessing her as a living sex toy rather than as an object of sexual desire.

The necropolitical captivity of B in this play reaches a tragic and frightening end in scenes 13 and 14 when B attempts to leave A but then again acquiesces after he swears to help her children obtain Spanish citizenship. B's last line, which she screams while being tied up, is "Júrame que no les faltará de nada . . . (*Pausa.*) ¡¡¡Júramelo!!!" (Swear to me that they won't lack anything . . . [*Pause.*] Swear it to me!!!) (*ML*, 70). Her trust in A to do the right thing is a terrifying reminder of how victims can be manipulated to believe that their perpetrator is a good person or a reminder that B has no choice but to trust A because he is her only hope. As A swears to B that he will do all he can for her kids, "La amordaza" (He gags her) (*ML*, 70). Unable to move or speak is how B last appears on stage, marking the final erasure of her humanity. Although it can be argued that she consents to the abuse, it is underlined by necessity and fear, as García Orellana notes earlier. Indeed, such an argument would be victim blaming, for her subjecting herself to this abuse is the only way she can protect her own survival and that of her family in a society that devalues immigrants as objects.

In the final scene, A alone appears in what appears to be a press conference, courtroom, or even a telephone call, explaining how he knows B, the mother of his clients.[18] He avers: "Sí, conozco a la madre. Contrató mis servicios para defender a los chicos por un pequeño percance que tuvieron en el colegio, hace poco más de un año. Su situación aquí es totalmente irregular y tenía miedo de que le quitaran la custodia. Pero el asunto no pasaba de ser una travesura de adolescentes, como pude demostrar sin mayores complicaciones" (Yes, I know the mother. She hired my services to defend her sons from a small mishap that took place at their high school, a little over a year ago. Her situation was totally illegal and she was scared that they would take custody away from her. But it all turned out to be nothing more than an adolescent prank, as I was able to demonstrate without any major complications) (*ML*, 70–71). From this quote, we know that a little over a year has passed since the end of scene 14, in which B was tied up and gagged to introduce her to "unos amigos, clientes míos, gente importante, con poder de verdad, no como yo. Les debo algunos favores. Y les encantan las chicas como tú" (some friends, clients of mine, important people with real power, not like me. I owe them some favors and they love girls like you) (*ML*, 70). Given A's alleged legal prowess as a corporate lawyer and his connections to powerful people, one could insinuate that he used B as a sexual bribe to tergiversate the crux of the case from rape to a small mishap, an adolescent prank.

After a brief pause, which indicates other voices that spectators do not hear, A mentions: "Me he enterado por la prensa. La he reconocido al ver su nombre en los periódicos" (I found out in the press. I remembered her upon seeing her name in the papers) (*ML*, 71). What exactly did he find out? A pivots again:

> Bueno, lo considero una cuestión de humanidad. Esta gente viene aquí buscando una vida mejor. La mayoría huyen del hambre o de las guerras. Y creo que debemos hacer algo por ellos. Ésta es una pobre mujer que no ha tenido más remedio que prostituirse para sacar adelante a sus hijos. Así que he decidido asumir desinteresadamente la representación legal de los chicos. Lo primero es encontrar a su madre. Pero he iniciado también los trámites y creo que no me será difícil conseguirles la nacionalidad. De momento voy a fijar una asignación, modesta, pero suficiente para que una fundación se ocupe de ellos. (*ML*, 71)
>
> Well, I consider it a question of humanity. These people come here looking for a better life. The majority are fleeing famine or wars. And I think we should do something for them. This is a poor woman who had no other option than to prostitute herself to provide for her children. Therefore, I've selflessly decided to commit to representing the kids. The first thing is to find the mother. But I've started the process and I don't think it will be difficult to get them citizenship. For the moment, I'm going to give them an allowance—a humble one—but enough for a foundation to take responsibility of them.

This pro-immigration speech is nothing more than a facade considering A's diatribes earlier in the play regarding the terrible life B would have if she left his side because she comes from such a horrible place. It is also a lie to declare that he is selflessly representing the boys, as B's freedom was the price for this representation. Furthermore, using a foundation to distribute allowances to the three children would, under Spanish tax code, allow him to write off the funds as philanthropic work and would absolve him of direct responsibility for them.

That B is missing presents two possible options: either she is locked up somewhere in A's home or he has killed her and her body has not been found. If B is alive, she is being subjected to inhumane treatment as the price for keeping her children physically and legally safe. On the other hand, if B is dead, then she has paid the ultimate price, as her life has been erased for the sake of her children. Furthermore, if she is dead, A in no way has to prove that he is upholding his promise to make sure that the children will not lack anything. Both scenarios exemplify necropolitical captivity in that B is stripped of agency and cut off from the rest of society, including her own children.

After a pause that indicates a question that spectators cannot hear, A says: "No. No, la custodia corresponde a su madre, por supuesto. Pero me aseguraré de que estén bien atendidos hasta que ella aparezca" (No. No, custody falls to the mother, of course. But I will ensure that they are well taken care of until she appears) (*ML*, 71). This would appear to indicate that the question is something to the effect of "Do you have custody?" By not taking custody of the children, A is once again able to distance himself from moral or legal responsibility. That spectators are only able to hear one side of the cross-examination of A represents the law as disembodied, inhuman, and easily manipulated.

The rest of the monologue appears to be an attempt to deflect questioning, perhaps by police, reporters, or lawyers:

> No, lo siento, no voy a hablar ahora de eso. Les ruego me disculpen, pero el objeto de estas declaraciones es otro. Los asuntos políticos siguen su curso en los tribunales y no creo que debamos especular con ellos hasta que no se dicten las correspondientes sentencias. Y permítanme recordarles, que todo el mundo es inocente mientras no se demuestre lo contrario. Muchas gracias. (*ML*, 72)
>
> No, sorry, I'm not going to talk about that now. I beg your pardon, but the purpose of these statements is different. The legal issues are ongoing in the courts and I do not think we should speculate about them until the corresponding sentences are passed down. And let me remind you that everyone is innocent until proven guilty. Thank you very much.

It is unclear what topic he is trying to evade, but I would propose that it has to do with his relationship to the missing woman. As a suspect in the investigation, it is true that he is innocent until proven guilty, but as spectators, we already know that he has committed atrocities. Due to the inside knowledge that spectators have, the final stage direction (*Un* flash *ilumina su sonrisa, que quedará flotando en el oscuro*) (A flash lights up his smile, which will remain floating in the darkness) is nothing less than terrifying, because it is likely that A will get away with his crimes unscathed and unbothered since his knowledge of the law and his connections would protect him from harm (*ML*, 72). The disembodied law is incapable of seeing A's acts, but we as spectators do. This dramaturgical strategy could be real as a means of humanizing us as spectators, in contrast to the dehumanized, disembodied voices of the law and of B. The play's ending pulls off the blindfold, allowing us to recognize inhumanity and therefore calls on us to render judgment and take action.

Mercado libre exposes the depth of moral corruption that abounds vis-à-vis immigration. Although exploitation is a trope that appears in many immigration plays (particularly in cases when the immigrant character is undocumented), the perverse nature of this play proves what José Monleón posits when he declares:

> Incluso los llamados derechos humanos corresponden a los que pagan, porque los que no tienen no son humanos, como prueban los centenares de negros y negras que mueren ahogados en el mar cuando navegan en busca de trabajo, o la mujer de nuestro drama. Todo es cuestión de precio. Es decir, de oferta y demanda. De libre mercado, que dicta la moral de las relaciones humanas, y se identifica, hipócritamente, con la libertad absoluta.[19]

> Even so-called human rights correspond to those who pay, because those without money are not human, as demonstrated by the hundreds of black people that drown in the sea when they set off in search of work, or the woman of our drama. It's all a question of price. That is to say, of supply and demand, of the free market that dictates the ethics of human relationships and identifies itself, hypocritically, with absolute freedom.

If those without money are subhuman, then race and class double-bind women like B such that they must become merchandise to acquire social and financial capital in Spain. In doing so, however, they teeter on the verge of becoming physical merchandise, as in the case of this play. Monleón's statement and the title of the play force one to consider the market factors that promote immigration and the way capitalistic values dictate interpersonal relationships. If the principle of supply and demand dictates interaction, then *Mercado libre* demonstrates that only those privileged enough to be at the top have any chance of prospering in life, and primarily at the expense of others.

Both *Los viernes del hotel luna Caribe* and *Mercado libre* debuted in Spain but were later performed in Latin America. Given the tragedy that befalls the immigrant protagonists in both plays, their international performances enact an extraterritorial form of border control by warning Latin American women of the dangers of Spain's lure.

Serving the Colonizer in Carmen Resino's *Unos pájaros verdes* and *Allegro (ma non troppo)*

Over the years, the public face of prostitution in Spain has shifted from Latin Americans to sub-Saharan Africans, and more recently, to Eastern European women. The caretaker/maid industry, however, has for the most part been consistently held by Latin American and Filipino women.[20] As Spain's population grows older, the demand for caretakers, home health aides, and so forth, has increased. In addition, as the vast majority of women are now active in the labor force, those with children depend on nannies if they do not have family members nearby who can help. In the majority of representations of caretakers, it is a Latin American woman tending to an elderly Spanish man.

Carmen Resino's 2016 play *Unos pájaros verdes* (*UPV*; *Some Green Birds*) demonstrates the effect that these foreign caretakers have on the elderly autochthonous population. The play is the story of an elderly Spanish man (Él) and his Latin American caretaker (Lusinda). The man's two daughters have decided to put him in a nursing home to stop having to pay Lusinda for staying in the home with him. The short play takes place on the day that Lusinda says farewell to Él at the nursing home. He tells her a story about how getting to know her changed his views on immigration, making an analogy to the green tropical birds that infiltrated Madrid. Many bird watchers feared the green birds would destroy the natural habitat of autochthonous birds, but over the years they have been able to cohabit the city without much disruption. Having been cared for by Lusinda for five years, the man feels indebted to her and tells her that he has written her into his will and testament as a token of his gratitude. Once she leaves, he has a bitter exchange with a staff nurse, Enfermera (Nurse). After kicking her out of his room, he takes a large quantity of pills, writes a suicide note, and drifts off to sleep, thinking about a dog and some green birds.

The play begins by providing the historical context needed to understand the relationship between Él and Lusinda, and why she would be at the nursing home visiting him. Él explains why he originally did not want Lusinda to come to his home: "Me apañaba bien solo. Con cierta dificultad, pero me apañaba" (I got by fine alone—with some difficulty, but I got by).[21] Concerned about his solitude as a widower, his two daughters hired Lusinda to take care of him and keep him company, but according to Él, it was all so that they would not have to physically take care of him. As he expresses to Lusinda: "Hoy todo el mundo está demasiado ocupado para cuidar de los ancianos . . . ¡Si no llega a ser por ustedes . . . ! Porque las de aquí tampoco quieren este trabajo.

Reconozco que cuidar a viejos no es muy agradable . . . ¡Y en cuanto a los hijos, ya lo ve!" (Today, everyone is too busy to take care of the elderly . . . If it weren't for you . . . ! Because Spanish women don't even want this job. I recognize that taking care of old people is not pleasant . . . And when it comes to children, you already know that!) (*UPV*, 211). The gradual abandonment of Él by his daughters is the catalyst for him to recognize one monumental contribution of immigrants: caring for Spain's elderly.

As Spain's population continues to age, and with so many younger people out of work due to the economic crisis, it is perplexing that there are not more Spaniards willing to enter the caretaking industry. Desiree Kleiner-Liebau explains that many Spaniards would classify such jobs as "3-D-jobs" (dirty, dangerous, demeaning).[22] Él reflects on this in his gratitudes to Lusinda: "Pero usted, ustedes, están ahí. ¿Qué sería de nosotros, de los viejecitos de acá, como ustedes dicen, sin ustedes? Ustedes nos cuidan, nos dicen palabras amables, nos sacan a pasear, limpian nuestras vergüenzas" (But you, you all, you're there. What would become of us, the little old folks from here, as you all say, without you all? You take care of us, tell us kind words, take us out for walks, clean our privates) (*UPV*, 212). The question Él poses is worth exploring because it is a philosophical argument in favor of immigration: What would Spain be without the immigrant communities that help the nation economically, socially, and culturally? Would there be a sharp decline in the elderly population if there were not a supply of foreign caretakers to look after them? Or would people like Él's daughters have to get into the trenches of caretaking for their own family members? The argument is often made that immigrants are parasites who do not contribute to society, but the level of intimacy required between the autochthonous elderly client and the immigrant caretaker is antithetical to that notion. Furthermore, as the former needs the latter to live comfortably, there is a certain vulnerability that must be acknowledged and reconciled.

The recognition of immigrants' contributions to Spain is symbolized by the fact that Lusinda is the only character (present or absent on stage) with a proper name. This decision reinforces her role as a catalytic agent of change in the life of Él, who symbolizes the Spanish "old guard" that was once resistant to immigration. The two other characters, Él and Enfermera (Nurse), are universalized, allowing for an extrapolation of their experiences to other Spaniards or Westerners in their same positions. The lack of proper names is a common trope in contemporary Spanish theater that facilitates translatability of a play to other linguistic and national contexts. However, Resino's deliberate choice to spell Lusinda's name with an *s* instead of a *c* is a subtle choice that is not easily translatable. Resino's spelling forces the Latin American pronunciation of the name, rather the dominant Peninsular pronunciation. This spelling is an example of what I call dramaturgical blackface, deliberate changes to spelling or grammar, or both, to indicate a character's Latin American origin that visually insinuates that Latin Americans and their Spanish dialects are inferior.

Lusinda means "illumination," which is very fitting considering her transformative effect on Él and his worldview. His ideological shift on immigration is explained in the story he tells about the green parakeets that he began seeing all over Madrid:

> Bueno, todo el mundo sabe que en Madrid, de la noche a la mañana, empezaron a venir pájaros de colores: azules, verdes . . . cotorritas, loritos pequeños . . . [. . .] Me dediqué a observarlas; no había confusión posible: eran verdes, tornasoladas, con un puntito rojo cerca de los picos. Había cientos de ellas. El trópico en Madrid. No dejaba de ser fascinante esa capacidad de adaptación. (*Breve pausa.*) Pero no todo el mundo las veía bien. Algunos decían que aquellas aves eran depredadoras, que acabarían con nuestros gorriones y con otras aves autóctonas, que llegaría un momento en el que todos nuestros pájaros terminarían siendo verdes y de pico curvo . . . Y durante un tiempo las miré mal, como al principio la miré mal a usted y a otras como usted y deseaba que se fueran, que dejaran nuestros árboles y nuestros parques y se volvieran al trópico. Pero las cotorritas se quedaron. Se han hecho fuertes, se han adaptado a los fríos invernales de Madrid y han proliferado, pero nuestros gorriones siguen existiendo. La convivencia es, al parecer, pacífica. Los pájaros de Madrid no terminarán siendo verdes como algunos y yo mismo llegamos a temer. Ahora me gusta verlas y sentiría si se marchasen. (*UPV*, 214–15)

> Well, everyone knows that in Madrid, almost overnight, colorful birds started appearing: blue, green . . . small parakeets . . . I spent my time observing them. There was no mistaking them. They were green, iridescent, with a red dot near their beaks. There were hundreds of them. The tropics in Madrid. Their capacity to adapt never ceased to amaze me. (*Brief pause.*) But not everyone was happy to see them. Some said that these birds were predatory; they would be the end of our sparrows and other native birds, and the moment would come when all our birds would be green and have curved beaks . . . And for a while, I held them in contempt, just like I held you and others like you in contempt. I wanted them to leave, to leave our trees and parks and return to the tropics. But the parakeets stayed. They've become strong. They've adapted to Madrid's cold winters and have spread like wildfire, but our sparrows keep existing. The cohabitation seems peaceful. Madrid's birds will not end up being green like some people, myself included, once feared. Now I like seeing them and would feel bad if they left.

The comparison between the tropical birds and Caribbean migrants, at first glance, is quite problematic, as it animalizes Lusinda and others like her.

However, the story serves as an analogy for how immigration can lead to a peaceful and meaningful cohabitation of different groups of people. Focusing on the Spaniard who is used to viewing Latin Americans as "other" and "less than," the story shows how he comes to see their contributions and accept them. Él, perhaps without realizing it, also dismantles the notions of assimilation and "contamination," as the native birds don't become green, nor did the parakeets become like the sparrows. Rather, the parakeets adapted to Madrid's cold climate, allowing them to survive in their new home. Similarly, Caribbean migrants have not invaded and overrun Madrid, but have adapted to the city and established neighborhoods and cultural roots in the city (e.g., the Cuatro Caminos neighborhood, which is heavily Dominican).

Lusinda's disbelief regarding her client's self-reflection only grows when he announces that he has amended his will and testament to leave her his beach house so she can build a better life for herself in Spain with her boyfriend. In addition, he states: "También le he dejado una cantidad de dinero. Pequeña pero le vendrá bien . . . entre otras cosas, para pagar a Hacienda" (I've also left you a sum of money. [It is] small, but it will do you well . . . among other things, to pay taxes) (*UPV*, 218). This gesture has the potential to completely change Lusinda's circumstances, as she will be a landowner with no debt to the state (which would likely aid her in applying for residency or citizenship).

Lusinda leaves Él after this announcement, to be replaced by the gruff Enfermera, who is rude and curt. Upon Lusinda's departure, Él prepares for his impending death by taking an entire container of pills with some water and writing a note. He then utters his final words: "Dicen que en un momento así es bueno pensar en algo agradable: en un horizonte infinito, en una playa, en un cielo azul, un perro que corre . . . y unos pájaros sobrevolando . . . Eso, un perro que corre y unos pájaros verdes . . . Algo muy relajante, muy tranquilo" (In a moment like this, they say it's good to think about something pleasant: an infinite horizon, a beach, a blue sky, a dog running . . . and some birds flying above . . . That's it, a dog running and some green birds . . . Something very relaxing, very peaceful) (*UPV*, 220). Él's suicide, which marks the end of the play, not only reflects a father's disdain for his daughters but also his admiration for immigrants (Lusinda in particular) and their support. It is telling that his final thoughts are of the green birds that he compares to immigrants. This shift in perspective over time is indicative of the power of individualized interactions as a way to combat prejudice.

The shift from prejudice to intimate acceptance can also be seen in Carmen Resino's 2006 play *Allegro (ma non troppo)* (*AMNT*). This comedy is the story of a bachelor musician named Paco (formally known as Don Francisco) and Marisela, his Latin American maid. Divided into three acts called *jornadas* (workdays), the play follows the dynamic between the two protagonists from employer–employee to lovers to antagonists to (perhaps) equals by the end.[23] I would agree with Luisa García Manso when she declares, "*Allegro (ma non troppo)* no es una obra de tesis feminista, pero refleja y revela de forma realista a través de la protagonista algunos de los problemas y situaciones ante los que se hallan las inmigrantes latinoamericanas en nuestro país, lo que constituye por sí mismo una reivindicación para su reconocimiento social" (*Allegro [ma non troppo]* is not a feminist play, but through its female protagonist it reflects and reveals in a realistic way some of the problems and situations that Latin American female migrants face in our country, which constitutes in and of itself an acceptance of their social recognition).[24] Despite not meeting the author's scholarly criteria for a feminist play, it is nonetheless an important work for providing insight into the lives of immigrant maids in Spain.

In *jornada* 1, Marisela arrives to find Paco's apartment in a catastrophic state and immediately gets to cleaning. While doing so, she plays the local Latino radio station and makes phone calls to her friends. Paco enters, dressed only in a towel, demanding soap and toilet paper so that he can shower and get ready for a long day in his study composing new music. Throughout the morning, he yells at Marisela to turn down her radio because it disturbs his concentration. At the end of the day, Marisela decides to enter the study to help motivate Paco by telling him that he needs to compose something with more heart and soul. He pays her no mind as they both go back to their respective tasks, but soon after he enters the kitchen and attempts to hug Marisela. This moment leads to a sexual encounter (between acts). In *jornada* 2, Marisela laments to her friend Jennifer that Paco has made no attempt to communicate with her since their encounter. What's worse is that at work, he speaks to her as if nothing occurred. Paco, on the other hand, is only thinking about the piece that he needs to compose, which is overdue. When Marisela enters the study again with suggestions, he loses his temper and tells her that her opinions about music are not valid because she never studied formally. He then proceeds to tell her that what happened between them was simply a chemical reaction, not love. Marisela takes these comments as a personal attack on her for being Latin American and thus tells him off before storming out. *Jornada* 3, which functions as an epilogue, begins with Paco on the phone with a colleague lamenting the fact that Marisela has not returned in the weeks since their argument. He says that he finally was able to compose a song, "Diez copas" (Ten Drinks), which has become very popular, and he personally dedicated it to her on her favorite radio station every day in hopes that she would hear it and return to him. Marisela suddenly enters the apartment and heads to the kitchen as if nothing ever happened. The play ends with Paco preparing a coffee for Marisela.

Similar to the case of Lusinda in *Unos pájaros verdes*, Resino employs dramaturgical blackface in *Allegro (ma non troppo)* to portray Marisela. At the beginning of *jornada* 1 when Marisela first enters Paco's apartment to find it an utter disaster, she exclaims: "La televisión *ensendida* . . . (*La apaga.*) todo tirado, embrollado, como si se soltase las pulgas . . . las chanclas ahí tiradas, las mondas sin tirar, los *seniseros* rebosandito . . . todito revuelto . . . Igualico que un naufragio!" (The television is on . . . [*She turns it off.*] everything thrown around, messy, as if one set loose the fleas . . . flip-flops thrown about over there, peels not thrown out, the ashtrays are overflowing . . . it's all a mess . . . Just like a shipwreck!).[25] Whenever Marisela speaks in the text, specific words are misspelled and italicized to indicate her Latin American accent. Dramaturgical blackface not only privileges Castilian Spanish as superior by mocking Latin American dialects but also further feminizes and racializes Marisela, given the gender and race dynamics of the play. Paco's Spanish, in contrast, is therefore portrayed as white, more masculine, dominant, and "correct." This strategy also suggests that Marisela's words are vocalized by people who speak Castilian Spanish. There is thus a double voicing here in establishing Castilian as dominant, for the words are vocalized by Paco on stage and by implied readers on the page. Therefore, both voices in the play serve to doubly center and underscore Castilian as dominant and superior.

The play takes place entirely in Paco's apartment, staged as three separate spaces: the kitchen, the study, and the living room, which is described in the stage directions as "una especie de terreno neutral" (a sort of neutral terrain) (*AMNT*, 169). This layout is demarcated along gender lines, as the majority of Marisela's time in the play takes place in the kitchen, whereas the majority of Paco's time takes place in the study. The gendered dynamics of scenography are magnified by the telephone conversations Paco and Marisela have with their friends and colleagues within their respective spaces: Paco only speaks to men and Marisela only speaks to women. However, both do make occasional references to people of the opposite gender in their calls. The telephone calls function as a way for the spectator to understand the protagonists' internal thoughts. Marisela's calls are to other Latin American migrants in Spain, which as García Manso explains, illustrates the affective network among Latin American domestic workers as they help each other to find work, housing, and leisure activities, and to overcome nostalgia for family in the homeland as well as the problematic men in their lives.[26] Marisela's calls allow her to supersede the limits of Paco's apartment by connecting her to Latin Americans across the city. On the other hand, the vast majority of Paco's calls are professional in nature, relating to the commissioned piece he needs to compose. The notable exception is his phone call at the beginning of *jornada* 3 when he declares that he is in love with Marisela. The development of gendered spaces and telephone calls at the extremes of the stage precipitates the coupling of Paco and Marisela, and foreshadows the ending in which the power dynamics shift toward a more equitable relationship.

Allegro (ma non troppo) consistently relies on traditional, patriarchal gender roles for its denouement to reach its dramatic closure. Although Marisela is relegated to a decidedly feminine domestic space, whereas Paco's space is concretely masculine, intellectual, and creative, the gendered discourse throughout the play is, ironically, held by Marisela. For example, when Marisela execrates men as egotistical scoundrels in her monologue in *jornada* 1, she notes two exceptions: Don Porfirio and Don Darío. As Marisela laments:

> Y [Don Porfirio] no era mala persona, no; no se portó mal con mi mamá, bueno tampoco bien, que no la recompensó después de todo lo que *hiso* por la suya, y tenía algo de falso, de viejo maricón *retorsío*, que dentro de los maricones también hay sus clases, como D. Darío, el médico, que aunque también *disen* se inclinaba por ese *lao*, era muy buen gente y nos daba gratis las medicinas, y no digo cómo me atendió cuando tuve a mi chiquitín enfermo a poco de *naser* . . . ¡Buena gente D. Darío! (*AMNT*, 174)
>
> And (Mr. Porfirio) was not a bad person, no; he didn't behave badly with my mom; well, he didn't behave well either. He never compensates her for all she did for him. And there was something fake about him, like an old, wicked fag, because among faggots there are categories, too. For example, Mr. Darío, the doctor, even though they say he leaned that way, was a great person. And he gave us medicine for free and I can't even express how much he helped when my little one was sick just after birth. Great guy, Mr. Darío!

This excerpt presents two examples of good men, among the many scoundrels she lists previously: they are both discredited for being homosexuals, however. Marisela's homophobic language implies that these men are less-than, despite being better human beings than the other men in her life. It is particularly telling in the case of Don Darío, who took meticulous care of her son, who is described as a good person even though he may possibly be gay.

These references to Marisela's gendered comments culminate in the play's inverted conclusion, in which she returns to Paco's apartment after disappearing for quite some time. When Paco makes coffee, there is an inversion of gender roles that appears uncomfortable for them both at first:

> PACO. ¿Le apetece un café?
> MARISELA. *Tá* bien. (*Haciendo intención de ir a prepararlo.*) Ahorita mismo lo preparo.
> PACO. (*Llevándola hacia el sofá.*) No, usted se queda ahí, quietecita. (*La hace sentarse.*) El café lo preparo yo.
> MARISELA. *Grasias*. Y muchas también por la por la *dedicasión*.
> PACO. (*Algo aturdido.*) ¿Cómo dice?
> MARISELA. Por la *cansión*.
> PACO. No hay por qué darlas. Se la debía. (*AMNT*, 221)

PACO. Would you like a coffee?

MARISELA. Sure. (*Making an attempt to go prepare it.*) I'll make it right now.

PACO. (*Directing her toward the sofa.*) No, you stay right there, still. (*He makes her sit down.*) I will make the coffee.

MARISELA. Thank you. And also for the, for the dedication.

PACO. (*Somewhat bewildered.*) What did you say?

MARISELA. For the song.

PACO. There's no need to thank me. I owed it to you.

Paco's desire to make coffee for Marisela demonstrates a move toward considering her as a romantic interest instead of an employee. His bewilderment at the word "dedication," however, implies that perhaps they still are not quite equal. This is because there is comedic ambiguity as to whether the word is a reference to the domestic task of making coffee (to be read as feminine) or the song he dedicated to her on the radio (to be read as masculine). She immediately clarifies, thereby keeping his masculinity intact. Even in this attempt to court Marisela by making her coffee, they both maintain the second-person formal (*usted*), connoting that in reality, Paco still maintains a higher hierarchal (and patriarchal) position over Marisela, because the usage of *usted* implies a distance between the two protagonists that contradicts the intimacy suggested by the scene.

The play's title provides insight into the key to a successful romantic relationship. The coffee-making scene exemplifies Paco's definition of love, which he outlines in a phone call to his friend Quique (diminutive of Enrique): "Pues como te decía, es una sensación como el de la salsa agridulce. (*Intentando bromear consigo mismo.*) ¡Allegro ma non troppo! diría yo" (Well, as I was telling you, it's a sensation like that of sweet and sour sauce. [*Trying to joke with himself.*] *Allegro ma non troppo*, I would say!) (*AMNT*, 219). This quote is the only moment in which the play's title appears. Translated from Italian, the musical term means "fast, but not too much so." In musical composition, the term is a tempo indication used for pieces that should be played quickly, but not overly so. *Allegro ma non troppo* is a common direction for the first movement of a symphony, which transitions to faster movements, such as in Beethoven's Sixth Symphony. Used as a metaphor for love, *allegro ma non troppo* could symbolize the desire to move quickly, but not to rush into anything too serious so as not to ruin the mood. Similar to the sweet and sour sauce metaphor, balance is the key to success. Given the polysemous title of the play and the use of music throughout the play to illustrate the protagonists' emotional state, the play's ending may indicate that the two will form a more concrete amorous relationship and leave their transactional relationship behind.

Unos pájaros verdes and *Allegro (ma non troppo)* put forth two arguments regarding Latin American domestic servants in Spain: (1) that their close proximity to Spanish men has the capacity to change the latter's perspective on immigration and immigrants, and (2) despite the transactional nature of the relationship between the Spanish employer and migrant employee, the former's vulnerability facilitates their compassion for the latter. Lusinda and Marisela function as neocolonial agents of change within their respective plays by culturally bridging Spain and Latin American, thereby allowing spectators to observe how their nation is changing as it simultaneously ages and becomes more diverse.

Return on Investment

This chapter has presented two contrasting approaches to the portrayal of Latin American women in Spain: tragedy and comedy. On the one hand, these women's migration stories are presented as tragic because the migration is one that does not improve their lives. The double bind of being female and Other creates the conditions for exploitation rather than the common male narrative of exploration. As seen in *Los viernes del Hotel Luna Caribe* and *Mercado libre*, sex work does not provide access to the financial capital required for the female protagonists to emancipate themselves from dependence on Spanish men. In fact, in both plays they are exploited to the point that only death serves as liberation. If the journey was worth neither the economic nor emotional investment, then what is the purpose of such a theatrical portrayal? Showing the horrors of migration to spectators creates empathy for Latin American migrants in Spain by demonstrating that they may not only be escaping terrible conditions in their homelands but may also be enduring similar (or worse) conditions in Spain. On the other hand, in the case of *Unos pájaros verdes* and *Allegro (ma non troppo)*, the migration is worthwhile because serving the *Madre Patria* (Motherland) (i.e., Spain) results in a better life. Although they endure standoffish treatment by their Spanish male employers, Lusinda and Marisela are financially and romantically rewarded, respectively, for their perseverance. These two women are able to ascend socially and financially, in contrast to the tragedy of necropolitical captivity that engulfs Yliana and B.

It is worth nothing that the two tragic plays are written by men, whereas the two comedies are written by women. Although all four are Spaniards, the gender divide presents an interesting juncture. Are female dramaturges telling more compassionate stories about women or is it that exploitation is considered par for the course when it comes to prostitution? I doubt either is the case, but the trend lends itself to interrogation. In these four plays, the female protagonists suffer from what Catherine Ross calls "quadruple discrimination—by being women, immigrants, ethnic minorities, and working in 'invisible' sectors of the workforce."[27] Curiously, not a single Spanish woman is present in any of these plays, though they are mentioned as a point of character comparison, such as Él's uncaring daughters in *Unos pájaros verdes* or the posh, indifferent women of Madrid in *Mercado libre*. The sidelined representation of Spanish women in these plays not only allows for the migrant protagonists to stand out in their own right but also falls in line with the representation of Spanish women in immigration films where they are portrayed as enemies of national progress. As Spanish women are portrayed as unable and/or unwilling to serve Spanish men sexually or domestically, migrant women supplant them in this capacity via prostitution and domestic service. At the root of this situation, however, is patriarchy, which belittles both groups of women (autochthonous and migrant) in accordance with their ability to serve. Race, Otherness, and immigration status serve to further denigrate Latin American women such that their service is invisible, thereby creating a system of postcolonial servitude that takes advantage of the cultural bonds initiated through colonialism.

Chapter 2

The Second Reconquista

Maurophobia and the Impossibility of North African Migrants in Spain

Historically, the Reconquista (711–1492) can be considered Spain's first national project: it entailed the national repression of otherness via the persecution, exclusion, and forced assimilation of the Iberian Peninsula's Muslim population in an effort to create a racially homogenous community. The aim of this centuries-long struggle, often known as the Muslim occupation or invasion, was to eradicate the Muslim "race" from political and geographic spheres.[1] The historical (re)telling of this era often paints a broad negative stroke about the presence and influence of the Islamic world in what is now Spain. After Fernando and Isabel conquered the city of Granada, the last Islamic stronghold, in 1492, Islam's influence in the construction of Spanish national identity was subsequently repressed and erased. Despite its monumental contributions to Spanish culture through architecture, language, music, and so forth, the Islamic world, Morocco in particular, serves as a historical and present-day antagonist to Spain. This antagonism is constructed in four ways: (1) the mythification of national figures such as Santiago Matamoros (the patron saint of Spain, whose surname translates to "Moor Killer"); (2) the carnivalesque remembrance found in festivals such as the Festival de moros y cristianos (Festival of the Moors and Christians), which takes place all over Spain, reenacting battles from the Reconquista; (3) Spain's desire to rebuke the famous phrase *África empieza/termina en los Pirineos* (Africa begins/ends in the Pyrenees), which depicts Spain as non-European as a result of its African heritage and influences; (4) the disparate ways the Spanish state interacts with Morocco as opposed to other former colonial states. One wonders how the constant reification of negative conceptualizations of the era and those connected to it is reflected in Spanish depictions of Moroccan migrants' experiences in Spain today. Moroccan immigrants are said to represent a second "Muslim invasion" as they currently make up 15 percent of Spain's migrant population, making them the second largest migrant group, after Romanians.[2]

Spain's 1985 immigration policy did not include Moroccans or Saharawis (people from Western Sahara) in the list of nationalities that would be able to enter the nation without a visa, even though they had been Spanish provinces between 1958 and 1975, and 1958 and 1969, respectively. This "ethnic filter," as Bernabé López calls it, privileged some groups over others, leaving those from the Maghreb (North Africa) mostly ignored in spite of its colonial connection and geopolitical importance to Spain. According to López, the ethnic filter created the conditions for undocumented immigration to Spain, which intensified in 1991, when "Se iniciarán las llegadas de las 'pateras,' que se convertirán en noticia casi cotidiana en los años sucesivos" (The arrival of *pateras* began, becoming an almost daily occurrence in the years to come).[3] This phenomenon initially was connected to Moroccans but later became associated more so with sub-Saharan Africans. The arrival of *pateras* to the Spanish coast greatly increased the number of undocumented migrants in the country.

Throughout the 1980s and 1990s, large concentrations of Moroccans could be found in the agricultural south of Spain, as López describes, "no siempre en las mejores condiciones de asentamiento, llegando a provocar reacciones sociales de la población autóctona como la que tuvo lugar en la localidad almeriense [El Ejido] en febrero del año 2000" (not always in the best living conditions, provoking social reactions from the autochthonous population like that which took place in the Almerian town [El Ejido] in February of 2000).[4] The El Ejido attacks in February 2000 were one of the most significant attacks on immigrants on Spanish soil to this day. In response to the stabbing death of a twenty-six-year-old Spanish woman, Encarnación López Valverde, by a Moroccan man, tens of locals destroyed immigrant premises, such as a mosque, a butcher shop, an internet café, and restaurants. Hundreds of immigrant dwellings were destroyed and dozens of cars were set on fire. More than three hundred immigrants were wounded in the almost weeklong violence in which local police did little to intervene as locals ransacked and looted immigrant homes and businesses. As one of the largest and most violent racist attacks in decades, the attacks of El Ejido marked a dark moment in race relations not just in Spain but across Europe.[5]

The tensions between Moroccan migrants and autochthonous Spaniards were exacerbated after the March 11, 2004, terrorist attack in Madrid (also known as 11-M). The public's understanding of the attack was manipulated by Spain's then president, José María Aznar, who for political gain in the national elections that were to take place three days later initially blamed the bombings on ETA (Euskadi Ta Askatasuna; Basque Homeland and Freedom). This was an attempt to conceal Aznar's role in stoking Al-Qaeda when he involved Spain in the Iraq War in 2003 against the will of the Spanish people. Two days later, foreign intelligence identified Al-Qaeda as the culprit of the attack.[6] Although Islamophobia was already increasing as a result of the September 11 attacks in the United States and the global efforts against the Taliban and Al-Qaeda, 11-M marked a turning point for Spain. Unfortunately, politicians used the terrorist attack to reify historical antagonism from the Middle Ages because, as David Moffette notes, "Anti-Muslim sentiments are still regularly expressed and the fight against 'Moors' is still mentioned as a founding moment in the construction of Spanish identity."[7] For example, in a speech he gave at Georgetown University on September 21, 2004, former Spanish president José María Aznar stated: "The problem Spain has with Al-Qaeda and Islamic terrorism did not begin with the Iraq Crisis. In fact, it has nothing to do with government decisions. You must go back no less than 1,300 years, to the early eighth century, when a Spain recently invaded by the Moors refused to become just another piece in the Islamic world and began a long battle to recover its identity."[8] This problematic retelling of Spanish history to an American audience inculcates fear and contempt for Islam and its followers (radical or not).

Aznar's 2004 speech is indicative of something more than Islamophobia because anti-Muslim sentiments hold historical weight that impacts the specific ways contemporary Muslim immigrants are treated. Ricard Zapata-Barrero instead avers "that there is *Maurophobia* [fear of the Moors] in Spain that has been constructed throughout history and that this picture is not a contingent fact but a substantive element of the process of Spanish identity building, without which Spanish citizenship cannot be understood."[9] Maurophobia leads to the invention of the Second Reconquista, the Spanish state's desire to disavow, reject, and expel those who are deemed to constitute the reoccupation of Spain because "The historical narrative that is constitutive of Spanish identity now recognizes the contribution and presence of Islam in the past, but not as Spanish."[10] If the recognition of Muslim Spain, Al-Andalus, and so forth, are to be understood as foreign to Spanish national identity, then as Moffette explains:

> This double bind of Muslim absence and presence contributes to the difficulty in considering Islam as constitutive of Spanishness in a way that is not articulated around the purging of the Islamic culture(s) of "Moors." It is in this sense that we can consider Spanish Muslims as impossible subjects, borrowing from Mae M. Ngai's (2004) analysis of the ways former colonial subjects become undesirable aliens through a historical process in which conquest, racialization, illegalization, and nation building are coextensive.[11]

Maurophobia thus serves as a way to understand the constrictive ways Spanish culture reifies historical racial antagonisms to push against the immigration of North Africans today. The construction of Spain's self in Hegelian terms is dependent on the rejection and disavowal of its North African history; contemporary North African immigrants and their descendants therefore unsettle the national imaginary and for this reason must be maintained in a state of perpetual Otherness or nonbelonging.

The antagonistic dynamic between Spain and Morocco is still embedded in the colloquial term *moro* (Moor). As Flesler explains: "Historically, the term *Moors* refers to the North African Muslims of mixed Arab and Berber origin that conquered the Iberian Peninsula in 711. In Spain, the term contains considerable affect. It is extended to signify any Arab or Muslim, and it has highly negative connotations."[12] Furthermore, as she continues, "When today's Moroccan immigrants are called *moros* [Moors] instead of *marroquíes* [Moroccans], their identity becomes symbolically collapsed with the concept of that attacking enemy" (3). This use of vocabulary incites a contentious relationship between Spaniards and North African immigrants. In addition, given Spain's constant desire to be seen as fully European rather than a nation with hybrid African cultural roots, the use of the word *moro* creates epistemological distance between its citizens and North African immigrants. As Susan Martin-Márquez astutely concludes: "In this sense, Spain is a nation that is at once Orientalized and Orientalizing. The dynamic resembles a Möbius strip, calling into question the possibility of any location 'outside' Orientalist discourse. For Spaniards, this positioning on both 'sides' of Orientalism—as simultaneously 'self' and 'other'—may bring about a profound sense of 'disorientation.'"[13] By referring to the immigrants as "Moors," there is a simultaneous and contradictory recognition and rejection of Spain's African history that produces autochthonous anxiety to this day. Aznar's 2004 speech simply politicized that dynamic for the world to see.

The year 2004 also marks Spain becoming the world's second largest receiver of immigrants, after the United States. That year, African migrants made up 25 percent of immigrants, 77 percent of whom were Moroccan.[14] The large demographic presence of Moroccans and the cultural antagonism it produces has been the source of inspiration for several playwrights from the 1990s onward. There is, however, a clear distinction between plays written before and after 11-M. Those written before the 2004 terrorist attack in Madrid depict Muslim characters as belonging to one of two dichotomous groups: those who have recently arrived from Morocco and those who have already established themselves in Spain and wish to quietly integrate into Spanish society. Plays written after 11-M, on the other hand, portray these characters as suspected villains who are guilty until proven innocent. As such, I have selected three plays to represent both historical moments: *Ahlán* by Jerónimo López Mozo (1997), *Bazar* by David Planell (1997), and *Ataque preventivo* by Juan Pablo Heras (2005).[15] The oscillation between these two depictions is fixed on the axis of perceptions of Moroccan identity as antithetical to Spanish identity, thus requiring the erasure of the former to obtain the latter. This erasure of identity is what I call the "Second Reconquista," a reinvigoration of the exclusionary tactics of the medieval era rooted in racist notions that have transformed, no longer considering North African Muslims to be a separate race from Spanish Catholics but rather a culture that is incompatible with Spanish/European/Western society. In her book

The Return of the Moor, Flesler refers to this phenomenon as the European discourse of "new racism," which "is especially pertinent in the case of Muslim immigrants, whose cultural traditions are seen as 'Islamic,' and therefore incompatible with the supposedly democratic, modern, secular values of Western Europe, a view that is shared, in its different national contexts, not only by the right, but by the whole political spectrum."[16] As she later notes, however, these culturally exclusionist methods are by no means new, as they date back centuries; I would propound that they have been refashioned to fit in with the rest of Western Europe.

The Picaresque Journey in *Ahlán*

Jerónimo López Mozo explores the intersection of race, migration, and criminality in his 1997 play, *Ahlán*. This play, composed of twenty-four scenes (two prologues, twenty-one scenes, and an epilogue), follows the picaresque journey of Larbi, a young Moroccan man who leaves his homeland in hopes of a better life in Spain. I refer to this play as picaresque because, similar to its canonical predecessor, *Lazarillo de Tormes*, the main protagonist is a young, lowborn man who makes a journey in which he is "mentored" along the way by a series of people until he reaches his final destination, in this case, Barcelona. In addition, Larbi, like Lazarillo, leaves each location in response to a tragedy. As Marco Kunz notes, "López Mozo optó en *Ahlán* por . . . mostrar a su protagonista en situaciones ejemplares y reflexionar sobre su condición de marginado y oprimido por la jerarquía social y económica" (López Mozo opts for showing his protagonist in exemplary situations and reflecting on his condition as marginalized and oppressed by the social and economic hierarchy).[17] By exposing the ills of immigration that unfold throughout his journey, such as capitalist exploitation, racism, and Islamophobia, Larbi uncovers a harsh truth of Spanish society. Even as the picaresque genre is seminal to Spanish culture, the *pícaro* immigrant is also fundamental to the cultural foundation of modern-day Spain.

The play begins with a conversation between a Spanish member of the European Parliament and a European commissioner in which they discuss the plans for the construction of a series of Afro-European bridges and tunnels between Spain and Morocco, which Spain will soon present in Brussels. As the stage directions note, "*Mientras hablan, en la pantalla aparecen proyectados mapas de la zona del Estrecho y perfiles del relieve submarino que van siendo sustituidos por bocetos de puentes y túneles y planos detallados de vigas, tableros, estribos, torres, péndolas y cables*" (While they speak, projected on the screen appear maps of the Strait of Gibraltar and outlines of the underwater topography that are being replaced by sketches of bridges and tunnels and detailed blueprints of beams, planks, brackets, towers, and suspension cables).[18] This is a fictional and hypothetical situation, but there is great value in understanding the concept of this project as a "nonspace," to use Marc Augé's term, which is to say that the construction of the bridges and tunnels would create spaces that are part of neither Europe nor Africa, and are thus devoid of cultural connotations, yet would serve to ultimately establish a sense of transcontinental camaraderie. For this reason the commissioner's reply highlights a cynical look into the European Union's geopolitical response to African immigration and Africa as a whole:

> COMISARIO. Me pregunto si los tiempos que corren son propicios para alentar empeños como éste. No es haciendo de pontífices como mejor contribuirán a la edificación de la nueva Europa. La tarea común es hacer lo posible por convertirla en una fortaleza. Hay que levantar muros en vez de derribarlos. Habría que buscar los pedazos del de Berlín y reconstruirlo a toda prisa. Entre el Moisés que abría caminos en el mar y el Hércules que creaba abismos apartando las tierras, hoy elegiríamos a éste. (*Contempla la orilla opuesta.*) ¿No le parece que aquella orilla tiene el aspecto de una herida abierta e infectada?
>
> DIPUTADO. Perdón . . . ¿Decía?
>
> COMISARIO. A ustedes, los españoles, les ha tocado ser guardianes de la puerta trasera de Europa. Pongan barreras que eviten el paso de la miseria que vomita el sur y recibirán nuestro aplauso.[19]

> COMMISSIONER. I wonder if now is a good time to encourage projects like this. It is not by acting as pontifices that they [Africans] will best contribute to the edification of the new Europe. The common task is to do everything possible to convert Europe into a fortress. We must erect walls instead of demolishing them. We should look for pieces of the Berlin Wall and reconstruct it as fast as possible. Between Moses who opened paths in the sea and Hercules who created abysses separating the lands, today we would choose the latter. (*Contemplates the opposite coast.*) Doesn't it seem as though that coast has the look of an open and infected wound?
>
> MP. Excuse me . . . You were saying?
>
> COMMISSIONER. It is the job of you Spaniards to be the guardians of Europe's back door. Put up barriers that prevent the passage of the misery that the South vomits and you will receive our applause.

López Mozo's ingenious usage of the word *pontífices* conveys two poignant messages. The word's etymology is derived from Latin: *pons*, *pont-*, "bridge," and *-fex* from *facere*, "to make." Thus, the commissioner elucidates that Europe should not make bridges with Africa. Furthermore, the word refers to the Pope, who in Catholic ideology serves as the bridge between heaven and earth. In this sense, the commissioner's disdain for the construction project as well as his desire to build walls serve to block Africans (i.e., sinful people of the world) from reaching Europe (i.e., heaven or the Promised Land). Spain's proximity to Africa via the Strait of Gibraltar makes it the perfect location to embark upon the creation of Fortress Europe. The notion of Spain as a fortress that protects Europe from the Global South has existed for quite some time. For example, Parvarti Nair's chapter on the border walls of Ceuta and Melilla clearly demonstrates that Spain's unique geopolitical position within the European Union has converted the nation, particularly the enclaves of Ceuta and Melilla, into a "third space" that is neither African nor European.[20] The symbolic framing of the fortress in this excerpt within the destruction and creation of divine barriers (i.e., by Moses and Hercules) connotes a superior Europe, one that is healthy and robust in comparison to the "open and infected wound" that is Africa. The use of medical metaphors also implies that Africa's perceived maladies (multiculturalism, miscegenation, poverty, disease, etc.) could infect Europe via the construction of such a tunnel, which would function as an artery moving goods and people between the two continents. All of these issues already exist in Europe on a less pronounced scale, however, demonstrating that the commissioner's exclusionist views function as what Balibar terms "prophylaxis," "the need to purify the social body, to preserve 'one's own' or 'our' identity from all forms of mixing, interbreeding or invasion . . . articulated around stigmata of otherness (name, skin colour, religious practices)."[21] This passage also highlights Spain's positioning between the two continents, which requires the deliberate appeasement of Europe to receive applause and continued membership in the geopolitical club that is the European Union.

Larbi's journey begins in Larache, a Moroccan port town, southwest of Tangier. When a dead body is found during a fishing voyage, one of the town's elders, Nachib, takes advantage of the morbid moment to publicly denounce the man who traffics migrants to Spain, Mimum Unacer. In an effort to silence Nachib's outcry, Mimun Unacer offers Jadicha (Larbi's mother) free voyage to whichever of her sons can kill Nachib. Larbi is charged with the task but is unable to do it, so one of his younger brothers finishes the job. As the oldest, however, Larbi is still sent on the voyage despite not being the assassin. Thus, as Kunz highlights, "La emigración empieza así bajo el signo de una especie de pecado original, el homocidio colectivo remunerado del que Larbi es corresponsable" (The emigration thus begins under the sign of a kind of original sin, the collective remunerated homicide in which Larbi is coresponsible).[22] The death of Nachib facilitates the journey but is also an omen of the struggles that Larbi will confront once in Spain.

Larbi's journey is foreshadowed to be arduous and fruitless even before he crosses the Strait of Gibraltar, because one's roots can never truly be transplanted. In the conversation that occurs before the murder of Nachib, Larbi tells him that by leaving, "Pronto aprenderé a vivir sin suelo y sin raíces" (Soon I will learn to live without soil and without roots) (López Mozo, *Ahlán*, 69). This phrase is stated to refute Nachib's notion that despite not being trees, human beings have their roots where they take their first breath. This abstract notion of roots and belonging do not convince Larbi, who is determined to "llegar al norte, donde dicen que la gente es limpia y noble, culta, rica, libre, despierta y feliz. Allí, aunque haga frío y el trabajo sea duro, está el futuro" (arrive in the north, where they say that the people are clean and noble, intellectual, rich, free, awake, and happy. There, even though it is cold and the work may be hard, is where the future lies) (68). To live without soil or roots leads only to starvation, though in the case of Larbi this starvation is felt through nostalgia, homesickness, racism, and marginalization.

The play's title, *Ahlán*, comes from the Arabic word for "welcome," which is certainly ironic considering the hardships and vehement rejection that Larbi faces throughout the play. The constant message is the exact opposite of "welcoming": the presence of Moroccans in Spain is unwanted and is thought to symbolically represent a possible return to the Muslim occupation that began in 711. In scene 3, Maestro (Teacher) and Guardia Civil (Civil Guard) discuss this moment in history and how immigration poses the new incarnation of 711:

> GUARDIA CIVIL. La dominación árabe duró ocho siglos.
> MAESTRO. La intentarán de nuevo.
> GUARDIA CIVIL. No lo consentiremos, don Claudio.
> MAESTRO. Esas gentes son testarudas. Cuando las expulsamos, hubo quienes se llevaron las llaves de sus casas por si ellos o sus descendientes regresaban. ¡Que pena de país, siempre agobiado por la miseria y la hostilidad del sur! (78)

> CIVIL GUARD. The Arab domination lasted eight centuries.
> TEACHER. They will try again.
> CIVIL GUARD. We won't allow it, Claudio.
> TEACHER. Those people are pigheaded. When we expelled them, there were those who took the keys to their houses in case they or their descendants returned. What a shameful country, always weighed down by the misery and hostility of the South!

The historical attachment to Spain and alleged entitlement to residence there held by Moriscos and their Muslim descendants are portrayed as an issue of national security, and taught as such to the Civil Guard member, whose job it is to patrol the coastline. Even more problematic, Kunz argues, is that "Esta visión comprende la historia como una eterna lucha entre civilizaciones antagónicas, como si éstas conservaran una inalterable esencia que siempre se opone de nuevo a la de sus antípodas, y así puede . . . hacer abstracción de todas las diferencias y ver en los inmigrantes magrebíes actuales sucesores de Tariq y Muza" (This vision understands history as an eternal struggle between antagonistic civilizations, as if they preserved an inalterable essence that always opposes itself to that of their antipodes, and thus can . . . ignore all the differences and see the immigrants from the Maghreb as current successors of Tariq and Muza).[23] The reference to Tariq and Muza is important as they were the Berber soldiers believed to have led the troops that crossed the Strait of Gibraltar in 711 to occupy the Iberian Peninsula. In addition, this perspective of Spanish history ultimately negates positive contributions that arose from the nearly eight centuries of Islamic influence in what is now Spain.

Scene 3 superimposes the past and the present through the use of historical interpolations to create a vision that forces the reader/spectator to reconsider and reconcile with figures of the Reconquista. For example, the Civil Guard's name is Rodrigo, a clear reference to Rodrigo Díaz de Vivar, commonly known as El Cid. One of the Reconquista's most well-known figures, El Cid represents the military prowess of Christian Spain against its Muslim nemesis. Rodrigo's role as a Civil Guard is to prevent the pending invasion to which Maestro refers in the aforementioned quote. Maestro also refers to his former pupil, saying, "Tu serás, como Peláez de Correa, azote de los moros" (You will be like Peláez de Correa, scourge of the Moors") (López Mozo, *Ahlán*, 79). This reference to another Christian warrior of the Reconquista only serves to emphasize the role that Spanish law enforcement plays in maintaining "Fortress Europe" free from Muslim occupation. In this sense, this scene reifies Flesler's claim that "the use of the rhetoric of invasion and specific references to the medieval or early modern Spain conjures up the stereotype of the violent, invading Moor and thus generates a reality that justifies the rejection of and the violence against Moroccan workers as a form of self defense."[24] Contemporary Maurophobia is the result of the nationalistic retelling of history in which the Moor is a looming antagonist, whose resurgence encourages and justifies marginalization and violence.

The Reconquista is often understood as a cultural and religious war, but over time it also undertook a racial component. The word *raza* in Spanish presently translates as both race (human) and breed (animal), but this first definition of the word is a result of the Reconquista in which Jews, Moors, and heretics were considered to be of a different "breed" because they did not follow and support the Christian theocratic power structure. This conflation of the concept of race with animalistic connotations of "breed" points to the nefariousness of the era for non-Christians and people of color in Spain, as white Christian Spain employed notions of "divine order" to justify exclusionary policies and violence against the "Other."

Scene 3 ends with the arrival of Larbi and several others to the beach in a *patera*. The stage directions clearly highlight that "*No se reconoce en ellos a los invasores descritos por el* MAESTRO *poeta, sino a sonámbulos contrabandistas de miseria*" (*One cannot recognize in them the invaders described by the poet* TEACHER*; rather, they are a group of miserable, sleepwalking smugglers*) (López Mozo, *Ahlán*, 80). The Civil Guard is able to recognize the difference, implying that the Maestro's lesson did not stick.

GUARDIA CIVIL. Están muertos de miedo.
MAESTRO. (*Devolviendo los prismáticos.*) No te dejes engañar por las apariencias. Fingen. Hay que empujarlos mar adentro.
GUARDIA CIVIL. El teniente dice que aunque sólo sea por razones de higiene.
MAESTRO. Por eso también. (80)

CIVIL GUARD. They're scared to death.
TEACHER. (*Returning the binoculars.*) Don't let appearance fool you. They're faking. You should push them into the sea.
CIVIL GUARD. The lieutenant says that even if it's only for reasons of hygiene.
TEACHER. For that, too.

Maestro is determined to eradicate Moroccans from Spain, even if that means murder. As Flesler notes, "since the beginning of this so-called 'Reconquest,' Spain has seen the effort at getting rid of its Arab and Muslim self—that 'rotten member of the Spanish body,' in Menéndez y Pelayo's phrasing—as a process that goes hand-in-hand with that of re-integrating into Europe."[25] Through this scene, López Mozo demonstrates that this deep rooted hatred and racism is taught through Spanish history and the veneration of figures of the Reconquista, establishing a moral and nationalistic high ground that is incongruous with historical facts. The rhetorical use of great medieval warriors to shape contemporary international relations is problematic and anachronistic at best, and racist and xenophobic at worst.

Larbi's first personal interaction on Spanish soil is with Juana La Loca, a Spanish prostitute who is obsessed with Moroccan men for their reputed sexual prowess and well-endowed members. She, too, uses Reconquista rhetoric to seduce Larbi to have sex with her. When Larbi states that he doesn't have money to pay her, she responds: "A lo mejor soy yo la que paga. Anda, enséñame el rico cuelgacuelga que Dios te ha dado. ¿Te da vergüenza? ¿O es que no tienes el arma poderosa como tus paisanos? Tengo medidas palmo a palmo herramientas impresionantes. Deja que palpe la tuya" (Perhaps I'm the one that pays. Come on, show me the lovely ding-dong that God has given you. Are you ashamed? Or is it that you don't have the powerful weapon like your countrymen? I have measured inch by inch impressive tools. Let me feel yours) (López Mozo, *Ahlán*, 83). The militaristic innuendos here serve to metaphorically praise Moroccan men, while simultaneously reducing them to their sexual organs.

The name of Juana la Loca is another significant historical reference in this symbolic modern-day consideration of the Reconquista. The daughter of the Reyes Católicos, Fernando and Isabel, Juana was given her nickname because after the death of her first husband, Felipe of Austria, in 1506, she is rumored to have gone mad. This mental illness led her father to imprison her in a castle in Tordesillas from 1509 until her death in 1555, allowing him, and later Juana's eldest son, Carlos I, to rule Spain in her absence. The relationship between the forgotten queen and the play's prostitute lies in their marginalized status, imprisoned objects of patriarchy, which may also explain her affinity for Moroccan men as the foreigners who may be able to set her free from the Spanish imprisonment in which she resides.

After being left in the middle of the highway by the trucker that Juana la Loca sexually coerced to give him a ride, in scene 6 Larbi finds his way to a Moroccan restaurant in Madrid owned by Abdul Jader. Before leaving Morocco, Larbi's mother had given him the address to the restaurant, stating that Abdul Jader would help him to settle in Spain. When Larbi arrives, Abdul Jader asks who else was given his address, to which Larbi responds that his brother Ahmed had received the same handwritten address a year earlier. As Abdul Jader angrily explains:

> ¡No! La policía encontró una nota igual en el bolsillo de un desconocido que apareció muerto no se dónde. Tuve problemas. Muchos problemas. Querían averiguar quién era y qué tenía que ver conmigo. ¿Entiendes? (*Hace trizas el papel.*) Llegáis tarde. Los tiempos cambian. Esto no es lo que era. Venís tantos . . . Lo invadís todo. Conseguís que se os odie. Y de rechazo a nosotros, que tenemos un sitio aquí y éramos tratados como personas. Nos atendían en los bares y los vecinos nos saludaban. (93)

> No! The police found a similar note in the pocket of a stranger who appeared dead, I don't know where. I had problems. Many problems. They wanted to find out who he was and what he had to do with me. Understand? (*Rips the paper to shreds.*) You've arrived too late. Times have changed. This isn't what it used to be. So many of you come . . . You invade everything. You got them to hate you. And consequently to hate us, those who have a place here and were treated like people. They used to serve us in the bars and the neighbors greeted us.

The tragic fate of Larbi's brother, Ahmed, not only endangers Larbi's chances for success, as border security has increased, but also endangers the possibility of peaceful coexistence for nationalized Spaniards of Moroccan descent.

Abdul Jader's fear of retribution is valid, because his racial and ethnic ties to those newly arriving have begun to outweigh his reputation as an established and honorable member of Spanish society. He tells Larbi:

> Yo tenía un prestigio. Era militar. Estuve en la escolta del Caudillo. Tú no has oído hablar de él, no sabes quién era. Un hombre con un par de cojones, aunque ahora digan otra cosa. Le apreciaba. Le veía cada día. Era un privilegio estar a su lado y saludarle. Lloré cuando nos licenciaron. Para entonces era brigada y tenía la nacionalidad española. Pude regresar a Marruecos. Otros lo hicieron, pero yo no.

> ¡Aquí estaba mi casa! La del pueblo, para ir de visita. Y eso, al principio. Luego, cuando no te queda nadie, ¿para qué? He vivido muy tranquilo hasta que empezasteis a llegar, hasta que aquel policía me hizo acompañarle a la comisaría. Me enseñaron el papel que traía tu hermano. «¿No es éste tu nombre y ésta tu dirección? ¿Qué puedes decirnos?». Y yo: «Sí, ese es mi nombre y ahí tengo mi negocio, pero no se de qué me hablan». «¿No será tu restaurante la tapadera de algún tinglado poco recomendable? ¿Cuántos empleados tienes? ¿Cómo se llaman? ¿Dónde viven? ¿Cuándo vinieron? ¿Tienen los papeles en regla?». Sólo cuando les demostré que serví al general Franco en la guardia mora, me dejaron tranquilo. Soy un honrado ciudadano que no quiere líos. (*Saca un par de billetes de la caja registradora.*) Toma esto y vete antes de que empiece a llegar el personal. (93–94)

> I had standing. I was a soldier. I was in the escort detail of the Caudillo. You haven't heard of him; you don't know who he was. He was a man with balls, although now they say other things. I appreciated him. I saw him every day. It was a privilege to be by his side and greet him. I cried when they discharged us. By that time, I was a warrant officer and had Spanish citizenship. I could have returned to Morocco. Others did it, but I didn't. My house was here! The house in the village, for vacation. That was at the beginning. Later, when no one is left, why bother? I've lived very peacefully until you all began to arrive. Until that policeman made me accompany him to the station. They showed me the paper that your brother brought. "Isn't this your name and address? What can you tell us?" And I: "Yes, that is my name and I have my business there, but I don't know why they've written it." "Is your restaurant the cover for some inadvisable scheme? How many employees do you have? What are their names? Where do they live? When did they come? Do they have their papers in order?" Only when I showed them that I served General Franco in the Moorish Guard did they let me go. I'm an honorable citizen who doesn't want any drama. (*Takes out a pair of bills form the cash register.*) Take this and leave before the staff start arriving.

Abdul Jader's connection to the Franco regime gained him access to acceptance by autochthonous Spain, but as time passes and the legacy of fascism fades into history, that connection not only depreciates in value but is even vilified. The national need to reduce undocumented immigration from the African continent to uphold the status of "Fortress Europe" and prevent the "misery of the South" from "infecting" Spain is very apparent in this excerpt. For Abdul Jader, who has been in Spain since at least the early 1970s, Spain is his home, but in the incident with the police, he was treated as an outsider.

Rather than engendering compassion for Moroccan immigrants, the situation spawned Abdul Jader's resentment toward the newcomers, who, as part of a Moroccan "invasion," he views as tarnishing his good name.

Ahlán was written in 1997, before the advent of fundamentalist terrorism that would lead to the global fear of Muslims now known as Islamophobia. At the time of its creation, the play portrayed the new wave of immigrants arriving in the 1990s to a nation that is not sure how to handle a surging migrant population. In scene 10, Esposo (Husband) reads a letter out loud to his wife that he received from Paris from his Tío Eulogio (Uncle Eulogy) back in 1982. This letter describes how the city of Paris became a multiracial city with the arrival of people from former French colonies:

> Al principio, pocos se dieron cuenta de que el barrio empezaba a ser distinto. Pero lo cierto es que las calles se iban llenando de morenos. Se movían con sigilo, procurando no llamar la atención para no alarmar a los vecinos. A la chita callando se adueñaron de las pensiones y ocuparon los pisos abandonados por inquilinos que veían con inquietud esa paulatina invasión. (121–22)
>
> In the beginning, few realized that the neighborhood was beginning to be different. But what was certain was that the streets were filling with brown people. They moved stealthily, trying not to call attention to themselves to avoid alarming the neighbors. On the sly, they took ownership of the hostels and occupied the apartments abandoned by tenants who anxiously watched that gradual invasion.

The letter, though talking about Paris in the early 1980s, could easily be referring to Madrid in the early 1990s. The demographic shift described here as a "gradual invasion," is nothing more than veiled racism. Once again, the rhetorical use of militaristic language connotes a dangerous dichotomy between the autochthonous and immigrant populations in which the latter is allegedly stealing from the former.

The letter then makes a metatextual reference that, unbeknownst to its writer and readers, highlights the hypocrisy of the "invasion" argument:

> Un paisano nuestro, catalán para más señas, que vive cerca de casa, ha escrito una novela que trata, según dicen los que la han leído, de lo que os vengo contando. Relata que, una mañana, al salir a la calle, el protagonista descubre que no sólo están pintarrajeadas las paredes con esos garabatos que usan los moros para entenderse, sino que el anuncio luminoso del bar que frecuenta ha sido sustituido por otro con esa clase de letras y también el de un McDonald's que abrieron hace poco. Advierte que incluso los rótulos de las calles están escritos

> en ese idioma de locos. Yo os digo que nuestro paisano no exagera y que, a este paso, no es ningún disparate liar el petate y tomar las de Villadiego. Pero me parece que no basta con mudarse de barrio. Toda la ciudad va camino de convertirse en bastarda. Si no llevara viviendo en París veinte años y si no tuviera la residencia francesa, os aseguro que regresaría a Madrid para quedarme a vuestro lado definitivamente. (122–23)
>
> A countryman of ours, Catalan, to be precise, who lives near home, has written a novel that deals, according to those who have read it, with what I have been telling you. It describes how one morning upon going out into the street, the protagonist discovers that not only are the walls painted with those scribbles that the Moors use to understand each other but the neon sign of the bar that he frequents has also been replaced by another with that kind of lettering, and the same happened at a McDonald's that opened recently. He warns that even street signs are written in that crazy language. I tell you that our countryman does not exaggerate and that, at this rate, it is not nonsense to leave home and flee. But it seems to me that it is not enough to move out of the neighborhood. The whole city is on its way to becoming bastardized. If I did not have twenty years living in Paris and if I did not have French residency, I assure you that I would return to Madrid to stay by your side for good.

The Catalan man to whom the letter refers is Juan Goytisolo, and the novel, *Paisajes después de la batalla (Landscapes after the Battle)*.[26] López Mozo's astute interpolation requires spectators to recognize the text and its satirical discourse. Goytisolo wrote the book to mock what he saw as ridiculous discourse in France regarding the arrival of immigrants, after the colonial presence of the French around the world. Tío Eulogio's inability to understand the satire, because he himself has not read the novel, means he buys into the fake hysteria that Goytisolo's novel presents. The hypocrisy lies in how the uncle ends his letter. As a migrant who left during the early 1960s of the Franco regime, he was once viewed in France as he now views Middle Eastern migrants. His inability to advocate for fellow immigrants reflects a European racism based on cultural, and more specifically as articulated in his letter, linguistic differences. It is also ironic that the uncle ignores the fierce rivalry and resentment between Madrid and Catalonia, regarding the novel's author as a countryman—he views them in this context as the same, united against the perceived threat of "difference." The disregard for Arabic is ironic considering that a large percentage of the Spanish language is derived from Arabic. Tío Elogio's hypocrisy also highlights how he perceives France to have an elevated status vis-à-vis Spain. Despite the alleged bastardization of his Parisian neighborhood, the benefits of his naturalized status as a Frenchman outweigh the purportedly disturbing demographic and social change of the "Arab invasion." Returning to Spain would not allow him the same benefits, because when he wrote the letter Spain was not yet a member of the European Union.

Upon rereading this letter, Esposo and his wife reflect on the contemporary demographic change in Madrid, which was also seeing an uptick in the Arab population. They depict this population as poor, savage, and potentially dangerous. It is for this reason that the scenic transition to their son is so flawless. Hijo, in his room, practices darts using the photo of a black man as his target. Wearing a large Celtic cross belt buckle, the spectator is made aware of his neo-Nazi inclinations, which become even more obvious when he sees Larbi's roommate Paisa walking down the street and he says, "Tengo curiosidad por saber de qué color es la sangre de los moros" (I'm curious to know what color Moorish blood is) (López Mozo, *Ahlán*, 125). This quote reflects the dehumanization of Moroccan immigrants in the eyes of Spanish neo-Nazis who view them not as fellow human beings but rather as an invasive species.

This chilling end to scene 10 foreshadows the hate crime that occurs in the following scene: the gruesome murder of Paisa, which Larbi (the only witness) recounts to Abdelkader. This murder exemplifies the reckless violence of Spanish neo-Nazis during the 1990s. A group of young men commit a senseless act and flee back to their homes as if nothing happened. Larbi, completely shaken by the experience, is unable to comprehend how or why such a crime would be committed. When asking about Paisa's body, Abdelkader responds:

> ABDELKADER. Todos los que mueren como perros van a parar al mismo sitio. Los hombres de aquí conocemos bien el camino. Lo hemos recorrido varias veces. En silencio, sin atrevernos a exigir que se haga justicia, pidiendo cada uno para sus adentros que el siguiente luto sea por otro.
> LARBI. ¿Tiene que haberlo por fuerza?
> ABDELKADER. Siempre hay quien cree tener motivos para matarnos.
> LARBI. ¿No hay lugar seguro para nosotros? (129)

> ABDELKADER. All that die like dogs end up in the same place. We men here know the way very well. We have made the journey several times. In silence, without daring to demand that there be justice, each of us praying that the next mourning be for another.
> LARBI. Does it have to be by force?
> ABDELKADER. There are always some who think they have motives to kill us.
> LARBI. Is there no safe place for us?

Sadly, the answer to Larbi's question must be no, as marginalization and violence follow him throughout the play. Abdelkader's reference to dogs (one of several metaphorical statements that compare immigrants to animals) only further illustrates the rhetorical ways "the other" is denigrated and relegated to second-class humanity.

As in other plays depicting neo-Nazi violence toward immigrants, the perpetrators go unpunished. This lack of justice becomes a psychological burden that Larbi carries throughout the rest of the play as Paisa represented a sense of hope in this foreign land, without whom Larbi resigns himself to accepting that Spain will never accept him. Through the picaresque journey, Larbi, just as Lazarillo, is able to see Spain as an imperfect nation wrought with social issues. Unable to cope, Larbi tries to leave Madrid but is captured in an immigration raid and sent to a Centro de Internamiento de Extranjeros (Foreign Internment Center), where he meets Masabo, a Senegalese migrant who overstayed his visa. Upon meeting, Masabo asks, "¿Cómo te han cazado?" (How did they catch you?), to find out Larbi's story (147). The use of the verb *cazar* (to hunt) is yet another reference to animalistic connotations in discourse on undocumented immigration. Migrants are hunted, detained, and then sent back to their homelands, as would be done with an invasive species. This subhuman treatment of migrants is often socially acceptable as the Spanish government foots the bill for sending them home, an act that could be read as benevolent. In addition, this "hunting" ritual fulfills Spain's role as the protector of Fortress Europe, preventing the passage of migrants into other European nations, such as neighboring France.

In scene 21, "La Mascarada" (The Masquerade), we observe two characters in the small living room of a Barcelona apartment: an unconscious white man (whose face has been painted brown with shoe polish) tied to a chair and Larbi, who wears a white mask made of poster board. Upon seeing himself in the mirror, Larbi tosses the mask on the floor and whitens his face with baby powder. When the man wakes up, Larbi explains that Hombre had drunkenly asked him, "¿Eres un moro de verdad o es que ya estamos en carnaval?" (Are you a real Moor or are we in Carnival already?) (180). Larbi, unfamiliar with Carnival, is told, "que son días en que la gente se disfraza y el mundo anda al revés" (they are days in which people wear costumes and the world goes in reverse) (181). This is a simplistic description of the Festival de Moros y Cristianos (Festival of Moors and Christians), in which people dress up as members of one of the two groups and battles from the Reconquest are reenacted. Larbi's detainment of Hombre serves to condense this role-play into a social experiment. His objective is to show Hombre, and himself, what racism is like from the other perspective. When Hombre asks why Larbi is abusing him, Larbi responds, "No te entra en la cabeza que alguien te escupa o te parta la cara porque sí . . . No puedes entenderlo. ¡No puedes! Y sin embargo, pasa. ¡A mí me pasa! (*Tapándole la boca.*) ¡Calla! ¿Te has sentido moro alguna vez? Ve haciéndote a la idea de que lo eres. Moro sucio, vago, ladrón . . . ¡Basura!" (It doesn't even occur to you that someone spits on you or pounds your face just because . . . You can't understand it. However, it happens. It happens to me! [*Covering his mouth.*] Shut up! Have you ever felt like a Moor before? Get used to the idea that you are. Dirty, lazy, thieving, Moor . . . Garbage!) (182–83). The problem with this racial experiment is that Larbi's victim did not racially attack him. In fact, all he said was the aforementioned joke about Carnival. Larbi's choice of victim is not personalized revenge, however, but rather revenge against racism itself, a system in which Hombre participates and from which he benefits. For this reason, upon untying Hombre from the chair, he says "Eres una buena persona. Por eso te ha tocado a ti" (You are a good person. That's why I chose you) (187). This premeditated violence is futile, similar to what occurs in scene 11 when the Moroccan migrants in the shanty town of Peñagrande choose not to retaliate against their white Spanish neighborhoods after their homes are mysteriously burnt down. As one neighbor says: "No convertiremos el barrio en un campo de batalla. Sólo perderíamos nosotros. Si se empeñan, nos borran del mapa. En otros sitios lo han hecho" (We will not turn the neighborhood into a battlefield. We would only lose. If they put their minds to it, they can wipe us off the map. They've done it in other places) (146). The rectification of racism in *Ahlán* is portrayed as the responsibility of the perpetrator. As immigrants and racial others, the Moroccan immigrants cannot be responsible for preventing the racist aggressions and violence committed against them. Therefore, although Larbi's racial role-play may cause Hombre to think twice before engaging in racist acts, it ultimately does little to improve Larbi's quality of life or ameliorate the conditions of migrants in Spain overall.

López Mozo's pessimistic approximation of immigration accurately portrays an immigration paradox: Is life better after migration? Larbi's picaresque journey ends in Barcelona in a state of resignation as demonstrated by the final stage directions: "*Larbi bebe otro trago y vuelve al trabajo*" (*Larbi drinks another drink and returns to work*) (203). Similar to that of *Lazarillo de Tormes*, Larbi traverses the morally corrupt trenches of Spain only to find himself still at the bottom of society. His racial circumstances circumscribe his experience and ultimately trap him. One could say that Larbi has grown and gained vast experience through his journey, and as he ends up with a job, perhaps his financial situation is better. However, there is no textual evidence to indicate the type of job that he has or whether he has achieved residency status, thereby highlighting his continued precarious status in Spain.

By using the picaresque as a narrative base for this play, López Mozo points out that despite good intentions, one's "bad origins" can determine one's fate. Within the Spanish imaginary, these "bad" racial origins date back to the Reconquest and the religious–racial politics that ensued thereafter. The plight of the Moor, the seemingly eternal antagonist of the Spaniard, lives on today through migrants and their children who increasingly form part of the Spanish population.

Identity on Display and up for Sale in *Bazar*

The vindicated rhetoric of the Reconquista has led to the creation of a sociocultural bifurcation for North African migrants: assimilate or drown in Otherness, by which I mean to say that those who choose not to assimilate (by giving up large portions of their cultural identity) are socially marginalized and automatically distrusted. This internal negotiation is the crux of David Planell's 1997 play *Bazar*, a two-act play that explores the inner workings of migrant identity while simultaneously critiquing the dangerous grasp of capitalism on human interaction in the form of catastrophe videos (à la *America's Funniest Home Videos* or its contemporary counterparts on YouTube).

Bazar debuted in Spanish in August 1997 in El Puerto de Santa María (Cádiz) and in English at the Royal Court Theatre (London) in November 1997 as part of its New European Writers' Season.[27] The play takes place over the course of two evenings in August in the Lavapiés neighborhood of Madrid, where Hassan owns a shop. The play begins with Anton, a neighborhood rabble-rouser, visiting Rashid (Hassan's recently arrived nephew) at the store to ask him to roll a joint as his arm is in a cast due to a bicycle accident. While preparing the joint, Anton presents a get-rich scheme: committing insurance fraud with cameras that were never really stolen from Hassan's shop to make money from the insurance claims. This plan requires Rashid to forge purchase receipts that Anton can then use to file a theft report at the local police precinct. As Rashid is undocumented, he wants nothing to do with the plan and brushes off Anton. Hassan then enters the store to tell the young men that a television program (*You've Been Framed*) has selected his video of Anton's bicycle crash, which he secretly filmed. Just for being selected, Hassan won 50,000 pesetas (approximately €300), which he agreed to split with Anton for his role in the film. If the video wins the grand prize for the best video the prize would be two million pesetas (approximately €12,030). Unfortunately, the program producers think the video was staged and ask Hassan to film a "better" version of the accident. This reproduction necessitates a recreation of the scene, its bystanders, and of course, Anton's bicycle crash. After multiple failed attempts, Anton is no longer physically able to repeat the accident, so Hassan himself decides to ride the bicycle, donning very Arabic clothing. This self-mockery is aimed at gaining the attention of the show's producers in a sort of racial schadenfreude (i.e., "Look at the silly Moor!"). Anton, feeling like the arrangement is not working out in his favor, demands a receipt from Hassan for the most expensive camera in the shop before consenting to help with the final take. Upon leaving the shop, Anton bumps into Rashid, who in turn steals the receipt and returns it to Hassan, explaining Anton's plan to commit fraud. Anton then returns to the shop to confront the men and demands the receipt while attacking both Hassan and Rashid. As a last resort, Hassan takes out the receipt and eats it. In a state of rage, Anton continues to beat Hassan and then shoots him with a price gun, labelling his forehead with a low price

(2,195 pesetas, or €1.32). After a barrage of racist insults, Anton leaves and Rashid rushes to help his uncle, who is badly beaten, scared, and has urinated on himself. The play ends as the two men stand in front of a mirror and Rashid tells Hassan how good he looks in traditional Arab clothing.

One theme that Planell dissects throughout the play is the fine line between integration and assimilation. Integration is the ability to function within the receptor society, whereas assimilation is the sociocultural replication of the receptor culture, which implies erasure of one's own culture. Hassan's view on these two concepts shifts over the course of the play. In act 1, he constantly pushes for Rashid to assimilate. On several occasions, Hassan chastises Rashid for hanging out with Mustafa, a young Moroccan migrant in the neighborhood who Hassan believes to be a hashish dealer. When Rashid suggests that his friend Mustafa perform the accident instead of Anton, Hassan rebukes him, stating: "You've been here three months . . . Are you going to spend your whole life with Moors? It's the same every day: you get together, roll a joint, you spend all day on your magic carpet drinking mint tea . . . Morocco in Madrid. Welcome to the ghetto. All you need is a photo of King Hassan on the dining room wall. Rashid, this is another country. People here live in a different way. Can you understand that?"[28] The transplantation of Moroccan lifestyle to Madrid is problematic, and even dangerous, in Hassan's eyes. It is this lifestyle, he says, from which so many are desperately seeking to escape, risking crossing the Strait of Gibraltar via *pateras*, or even swimming. Rashid, therefore, must "Forget that way of life. Forget that country" (Planell, Bazaar, 132).

One way to forget that way of life is to disavow one's native language. Hassan refuses to speak in Arabic, noting that part of adapting to a new land is to learn and use its language. In fact, he gets upset when Rashid tells him that Mustafa's father goes to Morocco every year: "Rashid, I've told you once, I've told you a thousand times. Don't you go speaking that Berber language back at me" (132). The original quote may not have the problematic tone that the English translation connotes, but it still transmits a clear message regarding assimilation. This anti-Arabic sentiment correlates to Hassan's views on Moroccans themselves, which surface in the volatile conversation he has with Rashid at the end of act 1. This conversation highlights Hassan's position on migration, its causes and effects, and his disdain for his countrymen:

HASSAN. I've been living here ten years. I used to go back, in 86, 87 . . . But then I understood. Here they live like rats.

RASHID. They? THEY??

HASSAN. Just saving, saving. And why? So they can go back on holiday once a year? So they can buy a Mercedes? Living here like animals, sleeping five in a bed, and going about there like big pricks in their Mercedes, which they drive around the village so everyone can see them, "Look, Hassan's got a big Mercedes."

(*Short pause.*)

HASSAN. Do you understand? And here they've got nothing. And there? What the fuck would I do with a German car?
RASHID. At least they have their family. But you. What have you got?
HASSAN. Don't get me wrong, Rashid. I'm not like them. I'm not like them at all.

(*Pause.*)

RASHID. Then who are you like? (132–33)

There are two contrasting positions on migration presented in this excerpt. From Hassan's point of view, it is not worth enduring slum-like conditions in Spain to boast once a year in Morocco. On the other hand, Rashid believes that those who return to Morocco have at least maintained a connection with their families and homeland. The distinction lies in Hassan's use of the pronoun "they." By separating himself from other migrants, he has assimilated himself into Spanish society and takes an "outside" perspective on Moroccan immigration. He is able to distinguish himself as a result of his relative financial success as a shop owner in the capital.

Act 1's forceful advocation of assimilation, itself a didactic maneuver, is contrasted by the verbal and physical violence of act 2, which leads to the reconciliation of cultural belonging and a rejection of assimilative practices. This shift is provoked by three events throughout act 2: Rashid's experiences with racism, Hassan's persistent desire to be on television, and Anton's attack on the two men. In the first case, Rashid experiences racism when a Galician restaurant owner (El Gallego) refuses to sell him mint leaves, to which Rashid retorts back fiercely and storms out the establishment. Upon telling his uncle the story, Hassan tells him a story of racism he endured in his first years in Madrid:

HASSAN. Six or seven years ago I lived in the suburbs. Thirty kilometers away. Every day I came in by train. One day two women got onto the train and sat opposite me. About as far from me as I am from you. I was reading the paper. The women were staring at me. Staring all the time. Then they began to whisper to each other. Bsbsbsbsbs . . . Moors here . . . bsbsbsbs . . . Moors there. Moors everywhere.
RASHID. Fuck. So you see what I mean?
HASSAN. Wait a minute. "It's just not right," one of them was saying, "The country's full of Moroccans." The ticket inspector came in asking to see all our tickets. And they just kept talking louder and louder. "They're taking all our jobs." I just couldn't stand this. They were talking about me as if I wasn't there. And the other one's saying: "My son's been out

of work for two years. It's just not right. Dirty Africans. Why don't they just stay in their own country?" Blah, blah, blah . . . The ticket guy was just behind us. One of them had got out her ticket. Just before he arrived, I leant forward, picked up her ticket and put it in my mouth.

RASHID. You what?

HASSAN. I ate it.

RASHID. You ate the woman's ticket?

HASSAN. The inspector came. "Tickets please." The woman was red all over, she couldn't even speak. The other one pointed to me, trembling: "The Moor ate her ticket . . . It was the Moor . . . the Moor ate it."

. . .

HASSAN. You understand? We have to think. Listen, we can live in this country, but we've got to use our heads and avoid problems. And we have to work. And anyone who wants to make it can make it. And anyone who wants to make a video for television can make it too. (135–36)

Hassan's rapid-fire response may have publicly shamed the racist women but could have brought him more headache had he been caught by the ticket inspector. Thus, his lesson to Rashid is that hard work, that is to say, meritocracy, prevails and ensures success for the immigrants who are willing to put in the effort. His utopian view disregards that his hard work is often viewed as theft by autochthonous Spaniards, as exemplified by the women's comments. In 1990s Spain, Moroccan immigrants, among others, quickly filled roles in much needed agricultural and construction jobs. As Spain's economy was for the most part booming, this influx of migrant workers was seen as necessary and positive. As the economy weakened, however, and particularly after the economic crisis in 2007, autochthonous Spaniards began to resent immigrants who had these low-paying but steady jobs.

The ability to make money quickly is a great motivator for many endeavors. Hassan's crash video is no different, but when he reveals that the television program has called to say they no longer have the budget to pay them for their video submission, he wishes to be on television regardless of the pay. As Anton refuses to repeat the scene, Hassan decides to ride the bicycle himself, dressed in traditional Moroccan attire. It is at this point that Rashid realizes his uncle's reason for not returning home: pride. In an attempt to convince Hassan to reconsider his decision, Rashid chides his uncle:

RASHID. Now I understand. You never go back on holiday. You don't want a German car. You want to go back on television.

HASSAN. Listen, boy, I can't waste any more time.

RASHID. Look at yourself. You look like a clown . . . You don't know what you're doing, or where you are . . . You don't even know who you are . . .

HASSAN. Rashid . . .

RASHID. They'll see it. You know that. You know they'll see you because over there, they watch Spanish television. We're not that far away after all. Are we? Isn't that how you're thinking of going back? Going back to your own country? In a television channel? Playing the clown on television? Hassan, how old are you?

HASSAN. Kh'Rey, kh'Rey, Rashid. Men H'na. Men H'na. (*Leave. Get out of here.*)

RASHID. You've got it all wrong, Hassan. You need help. (160–61)

To appear on television for a second time would bestow Hassan with "fifteen minutes of fame," which would be sufficient for him to show those back in Tangier that he is successful. For this reason, he never returns home because the ostentation of returning in a German car is nothing in comparison to the widespread appeal of a television appearance. Hassan's fame, however, comes at the expense of his Moroccan identity, which he wears as a carnivalesque mask aimed at entertaining the autochthonous viewership. This buffoonery, similar to that of the black caricatures that would "shuck and jive" audiences in the United States, does nothing to improve the antagonistic state of affairs between autochthonous Spaniards and immigrating Moroccans. In fact, his appearance would only serve to perpetuate stereotypes and prejudices.

These prejudices surface at the end of the play when Anton attacks Hassan for the camera receipt that Rashid slyly stole from his pocket. While threatening Hassan, Anton repeatedly calls him Mahomet (a variant of Muhammad). Overcome with fear, Hassan reverts to speaking Arabic:

ANTON. Mahomet, you'd better give me that fucking receipt before I lose patience. Mahomet, give me the receipt or I'll fucking lose my temper!

HASSAN. Ismi Hasan, machi Muhammad (*My name's Hassan, not Muhammad.*)

ANTON. I think you owe me an apology.

HASSAN. Magadish nat'leb esmah. (*I'm not going to say I'm sorry.*)

ANTON. Listen, talk Christian or we're not going to understand each other. (163–64)

Up until this point, Anton appears to be antiracist, but the physical pain he has endured and the lack of compensation are the last straw, causing him to erupt with racist vehemence. The repetition of the name "Muhammad," a venerated name in Islam, serves as a denigration of Hassan's Islamic heritage.

The protagonists' names reveal deeper meanings in the plot. "Hassan" comes from the Arabic for "handsome," Rashid comes from the Arabic for "rightly guided," and Anton is derived from Latin meaning "he who confronts his adversaries." Hassan's vain pursuit of television fame through the destruction and parody of his Moroccan identity is thwarted only through Rashid's guidance. Anton therefore serves as the adversary who must be vanquished in order for Hassan's delusion of Spanish assimilation to be defeated.

It is not until Anton attacks Hassan and Rashid that Hassan comes to terms with his Otherness in Spain. In an effort to spite Anton and prove to Rashid that he can stand up for his people, Hassan eats the camera receipt, causing Anton to shoot at him with a price gun:

> ANTON. Filthy son of a bitch. Swallowed the receipt . . . I'm going to shoot you, fucker. I'm going to shoot you in your Jewish Arab Moorish son of a shitty bitch head.
>
> (*Anton picks up the price gun that fires little sticky labels with the prices on them. He goes back to Hassan.*)
>
> And there you have it, the only language you understand. Let's have a look at the market price.
>
> (*He fires at Hassan's forehead.*)
>
> ANTON. Mahomet you cunt you're worth two thousand one hundred and ninety five. That's cheap, cunt. That's a bargain. (165)

Anton's use of slurs not only invokes the racist rhetoric of the Reconquista by referencing Jews, Arabs, and Moors, but also serves to emasculate and dehumanize Hassan by likening him to a product worth very little (approximately €13). Anton also tries to denigrate him by calling him the curse word for female sexual genitalia, patriarchally viewed as a passive object, a vacant receptacle to be filled and used by male penile power—notably, it is an attitude common to both Spanish and Moroccan culture. The destruction of the receipt, foiling Anton's plan to commit insurance fraud, defuses Anton such that he storms out of the shop, finally putting an end to the television show madness that occupies much of act 2.

In the final exchange of the play, Rashid walks Hassan over to a mirror so that he can observe how much better Moroccan clothes suit him:

> RASHID. Come and look.
>
> (*Rashid takes Hassan to a mirror.*)
>
> There. What do you think?
>
> HASSAN. Think of what?
> RASHID. The djellaba. It really suits you.
> HASSAN. Does it?

(*Rashid puts on his slippers.*)

RASHID. And African slippers. You should try them. They're much more comfortable.
HASSAN. Do you think so?

(*Hassan looks at himself in the mirror. He thinks about it.*

Fade to black.) (166–67)

In this final dialogue, Rashid serves as a guide, bringing Hassan back to his African roots. The contemplation of his Moroccan roots in this excerpt disavows the assimilationist stance Hassan had at the beginning of the play. His oscillation is ultimately caused by the racist violence that Anton inflicts on him, causing him to reflect on his identity and his sense of belonging in Spain. Rashid, on the other hand, is fully aware that Spain does not accept him for who he is and thus keeps his guard up except when with other Moroccans, such as his friend Mustafa. The violent attack brings family together but also solidifies their sense of identity and pride. Violence is portrayed to the audience as a product of Spain (Anton) rather than of its immigrants (Hassan and Rashid).

Bazar powerfully portrays the internal cultural struggle of Moroccan migrants, who may feel compelled to erase their cultural identity to assimilate into Spanish society. As the play makes clear, this erasure does not prevent Spaniards from perceiving otherness in Moroccan migrants and exhibiting prejudice toward them, thereby resulting in their marginalization despite linguistic and cultural fluency. Hassan's transformation throughout the play, culminating in the reacceptance of his Moroccan garb and the language and culture that come with it, can therefore be interpreted in two ways. From a positive perspective, one could claim that this ending portrays that immigrants should not have to change who they are to be accepted in Spain. A pessimistic interpretation, however, would argue that Moroccanness is forever deemed antithetical to Spanish national identity given that Anton is never punished for his racist attack on Hassan and can continue committing insurance fraud, perhaps at the expense of other migrant store owners. In addition, Planell's critiques of assimilation are superimposed on a critique of the cultural phenomenon that is "trash television," which in 1997 predates the advent of reality television and the effects it has had on global society. Hassan's desperate desire for acceptance and fame in Spain through which he can grandstand to those back in Morocco, coupled with his capitalistic desire to win the prize for best video make for a dangerous combination in *Bazar*. In this way, Planell correlates the pathological desire to assimilate with the desperation for fame and wealth, concluding that such a pursuit results in the loss of oneself.

Unfounded Suspicion in *Ataque preventivo*

The March 11, 2004, terrorist attack in Madrid shifted Spanish conceptualizations of terrorism from an internal conflict (ETA, the often-violent Basque separatist group) to an external conflict (Al-Qaeda, a fundamentalist Muslim terrorist group). The Spanish government first erroneously blamed ETA as the culprit of the attack, which was largely seen as a political ploy since the national elections were to be held on March 14. Global intelligence agencies refuted that claim by providing evidence for Al-Qaeda involvement in the blasts. Not only did the deceit lead to the electoral defeat of the ruling Partido Popular; it also sparked nationwide Islamophobia, similarly to that seen in the United States and France after similar attacks. This irrational fear then fixed itself on the faces of the growing North African population in Spain. It is exactly this phobia that Juan Pablo Heras explores in his 2005 play *Ataque preventivo*. As the title suggests, there is a preventive attack on a Middle Eastern man in the first-class cabin of a plane flying from Cairo to Madrid, which leads to his death. This attack is justified by passengers' irrational (and racist) fears that the man may be a terrorist threat to flight safety.

Although the play was published shortly after the 11-M attack in 2004, Heras explained to me via email that he took the concept of the preventive attack from the military policy of George W. Bush. The United States' wars against Al-Qaeda in Iraq and Afghanistan, spurred by the gruesome events of September 11, 2001, were preventive wars sold to the nation as necessary for national security. President Bush stated in the now famous 2002 "Bush Doctrine," "We must be prepared to stop rogue states and their terrorist clients before they are able to threaten or use weapons of mass destruction against the United States and our allies and friends."[29] History, though, has revealed that the motivations for these wars were not as well intentioned as they were marketed to be to the American public. In a similar fashion, Heras is able to spotlight the ways preconceived notions of various groups of peoples lead to prejudices and racism that collide in a fatal manner.

According to the playwright, the play is a "puzzle dramático de 31 piezas, ligadas por medio de seis ejes a los personajes centrales y al único espacio que comparten: el avión. Entre paréntesis se indica el orden cronológico de la acción, evidentemente distinto al propuesto para la escena. La presentada, aun siendo la preferida por el autor, no es sino una opción más de ordenación de las piezas" (dramatic puzzle composed of thirty-one pieces linked by means of six axes to the main characters and the only space they share: the airplane. The chronological order of the action is indicated in parentheses. The presented option, even being the author's preferred order, is nothing more than one more option to order the pieces).[30] Many have assumed that this narrative structure is inspired by Julio Cortázar's 1963 novel *Rayuela* (*Hopscotch*), which institutionalized the genre we know in English as the "choose your own adventure" novel. Heras explains, rather, that his inspiration for *Ataque preventivo* is

Mexican playwright Hugo Salcedo's 1989 play *El viaje de los cantores* (*The Crossing*).[31] Salcedo's play chronicles the true journey of a group of Mexican migrants who die via asphyxiation as a result of being trapped in the sealed wagon of a train crossing the border into the United States.[32] According to Salcedo's staging notes, he suggests three ways to organize the play's ten scenes: chronologically, the published order, or a randomly selected order before each night's performance.[33] The ability to scramble the scenes establishes a continual prism through which to understand and interpret the work.

Heras's puzzle is a bit more complex as it uses a structure in which the story lines of Claudia, Sonia, Emma and Carlos, López, and Rachid function as spokes (five sets of five scenes numbered 1–5 according to their chronological order) that portray what happened in their lives leading up to the fateful flight. These five individual story lines converge in the remaining six scenes, numbered 1–6 according to the chronological order of events that take place on the plane, starting from the moment when Rachid is pronounced dead. Heras suggests an order of scenes but gives liberty to directors to change it to their liking (*AP*, 15–16). As the five individual story lines occur parallel to each other, a true chronological order is not possible. Therefore, *Ataque preventivo*, through the use of a puzzle-like narrative structure, forces the spectator/reader to unravel the details of the mystery of Rachid's death in the first-class cabin of the plane, as well as the lives of the other passengers with whom he flew.

It is necessary to outline each of the individual story lines to understand how these characters interact during the six scenes on board the plane. Claudia's story line begins with a dialogue with her agent Andrés regarding how she must give up everything and everyone in her life the moment she becomes famous. Some years later, Claudia's friend Sandra asks her for an autograph for her daughter, also named Claudia. They try to catch up, but it is clear that too much time has passed for their friendship to have the affectionate connection it once had. In Claudia scene 3, her agent Andrés tells her that she is losing fame as she has not debuted or sold new paintings in months. Desperate and anxious, Claudia asks Andrés for drugs, which he gives her with the condition that he gets a new painting by the next evening. In Claudia scene 4, Sandra has just been hired as a flight attendant and talks about stability. Claudia mentions that she will have an exposition in New York in two months but has not signed the contract. In Claudia's fifth scene, her agent wants to know why Claudia has not been home in months to paint. She responds that she will return to painting when she feels more secure, having saved enough to feel stable. She then boards her flight to Cairo where she will stay for a night before returning to Madrid.

Claudia's story line presents a commentary on the capitalistic frenzy in the world of the fine arts. As a painter, she is at the mercy of word of mouth to determine the value of her work. The subjectivity of her profession creates an anxiety that she is only capable of conquering through the use of drugs.

While her job allows her to travel the world for expositions, the pressure to produce groundbreaking work overwhelms her. The stress causes her to change careers and become a flight attendant so she can have more financial stability and literally live in the clouds that she once inhabited on earth through painting and drugs.

Stress and anxiety affect the play's youngest character, Sonia, in very different ways. Her story line begins with a scene in which at the age of nine she asks her parents if she can go ride bicycles at her friend Dani's house. Her mother explains that Dani may have offered to lend her a bicycle, "pero una cosa es lo que se dice para no molestar a la gente y otra cosa lo que piensa" (what people say out of kindness is one thing but what they think is another) (*AP*, 36). This lesson manifests itself at the age of sixteen when she does not wish to engage in sexual relations with the boy she is seeing because she is afraid of the risk of the relationship going sour in the future. Her risk aversion transforms into anxiety attacks that she discusses at age eighteen with a friend while smoking marijuana. Sonia's friend gives her pepper spray, because "Esto es la libertad. . . . Es una cosa muy simple. Es como un insecticida. No. Es un insecticida. Pero lo que matas son mosquitos de un metro ochenta" (This is your freedom. . . . It's easy to use. It's like insect repellent. It is a repellent. But what you're killing is six-foot-tall mosquitos) (*AP*, 63–64). Men are the obstruction to Sonia's ability to live anxiety-free. The ability to repel gives Sonia the will to choose with whom she wishes to spend her time, consensually. Four years later, she is a more independent woman, telling her parents that she has booked a flight to Egypt with her university girlfriends to stay with a host family. Once again, her mother objects to her claim that the host family actually wants them there with a phrase eerily similar to that which appears in scene 1, stating, "pero una cosa es lo que se hace por hospitalidad, y otra lo que se piensa. Igual sienten que les estáis molestando" (being hospitable is one thing but what they actually think is another. They still might think you're disturbing them) (*AP*, 88). Sonia's mother is an embodiment of the Spanish fear of *lo que dirán*, a constant adjustment of one's life according to what others will think or say about you. Although she thinks she is protecting her daughter, this leaves Sonia sheltered and thus more vulnerable to risks that set off anxiety attacks.

Rather than shelter her, Sonia's father sees the trip as a waste of money and time since there are Arabs who live in her neighborhood. His response to her desire to go Egypt foreshadows Spanish attitudes toward North Africans that appear in discussions on board the plane:

PADRE. Yo no sé qué interés tienes en ir para allá. ¿Es que no ves árabes todos los días en tu propio barrio?

SONIA. Papá . . .

PADRE. No, hija, no quiero decir que me parezca mal. No tengo nada contra los árabes. De hecho, sabes que tengo un amigo árabe.

SONIA. ¿Y?
PADRE. Es que no le veo el interés al viaje. No sé qué tiene de especial. (*AP*, 88)

FATHER. I don't know what appeals to you about going there. Don't you see enough Arabs in your own neighborhood?
SONIA. Dad . . .
FATHER. No, love, I'm not saying that there's anything wrong with that. I've got nothing against Arabs. And you know I've got a friend who's an Arab.
SONIA. So?
FATHER. I just don't see why you're interested in this trip. I don't see what's so special about it.

This excerpt harkens back to Tío Elogio's letter in *Ahlán*, as Sonia's father shows resentment toward the Arabs who live in the neighborhood. Her father's attempt to defuse his racist rhetoric by saying he has an Arab friend is thwarted by Sonia, such that he must come up with another reason for why she shouldn't go to Egypt: there is nothing special to see there. To discredit Egypt as an uninteresting travel location for no other reason than it being an Arab nation is racist and lazy logic. To cite security concerns would be more valid, especially given Sonia's anxiety around unknown men.

In her final individual scene, Sonia is in Egypt talking on the phone to the girlfriend back in Spain who gave her the pepper spray. Sonia explains that her friends Diana and Sara deviated from the route and tour guide, and she, averse to the risk, chose not to follow them and is walking to her hotel without them. She then describes a street encounter with an Egyptian man:

> Hubo un chico. (. . .) No, tonta, fue de lejos. Un chico muy moreno con los ojos muy azules. (. . .) Sí, egipcio, pero egipcio raro. No sé. Como un ángel. Sí. Me miró. Y hasta creo que me siguió. (. . .) Sí, llevaba el spray. Pero no lo llevaba a mano, y no sé por qué, ni siquiera lo saqué del fondo del bolso. No me daba miedo. No sé, no sé cómo explicarlo. Ya te digo. Como un ángel. (*Ríe.*) Idiota . . . ¿Te imaginas? (. . .) No. Es peligroso. Es peligroso alejarse del guía. Es poco recomendable cuando te vas de viaje, y más a países como éste. (*AP*, 23)

> There was a guy. (. . .) No, stupid, just from a distance. A guy with dark skin but really blue eyes. (. . .) Yeah, Egyptian, but not your typical Egyptian (. . .) I don't know. Like an angel. (. . .) Yeah. He looked at me. And then I think he followed me. (. . .) Yeah, I had my spray with me. But I didn't have it in my hand, and I don't know why, but I didn't even dig it out of my bag. I wasn't afraid of him. I don't know how to explain it. As I said before, he was like an angel. (*Laughing.*)

> You idiot . . . Can you imagine? (. . .) No. It's dangerous to leave the guide when you travel, especially in countries like that.

Sonia is simultaneously attracted to and scared of this man. His beauty throws her off, signaling her Western notions of beauty; she is unable to fathom a dark-skinned man with blue eyes and thus deems him "not your typical Egyptian." Sonia's encounter with desire in Egypt leaves her uncomfortable with herself because she wanted to stray from the guided itinerary to pursue him but believes in "countries like that" it would be unsafe. The anxiety of the situation provokes her desire to be "ya en el avión. Volando. Lejos de todo" (already on the plane home. Flying. Away from everything) (*AP*, 23).

On the other hand, López, does not wish to keep flying. He seeks tranquility, but the cutthroat competition of his job begets chaos. In his first scene, López speaks to El Aliado (The Accomplice) about rumors that his coworker Muñoz may try to usurp his job. In efforts to get Muñoz out of his life, López offers him a job as the head of the Chinese division of the company:

> MUÑOZ: ¿Por qué yo?
> LÓPEZ: Porque te lo mereces, Muñoz. Es justo lo que te mereces.
> MUÑOZ: No me lo esperaba. ¿Cómo ha surgido esto?
> LÓPEZ: Yo mismo te recomendé. Tengo mis razones.
> MUÑOZ: Lo pensaré esta noche, y mañana . . .
> LÓPEZ: No. No hay nada que pensar. Es la oportunidad de tu vida. Algo único. Escúchame. Te diré una cosa: no me gustaría que te arrepintieras durante toda la vida de haber dejado pasar esta oportunidad. ¿Entiendes? (*AP*, 56)

> MUÑOZ: Why me?
> LÓPEZ: Because you deserve it, Muñoz. It's exactly what you deserve.
> MUÑOZ: I wasn't expecting this. How did all this come about?
> LÓPEZ: It was me who recommended you. I've got my reasons.
> MUÑOZ: I'll sleep on it, and tomorrow . . .
> LÓPEZ: There's nothing to sleep on. This is the chance of a lifetime. A once in a lifetime opportunity. Listen to me. I'll tell you something: I'd hate you to turn down this opportunity and then regret it for the rest of your life. Do you understand?

López's ill-intentioned reasoning presented as a life-changing opportunity is an offer that Muñoz cannot refuse. With Muñoz out of the picture, however, López has to keep up with the demands of his job alone. In his third scene, López frenetically makes four phone calls, all while sniffing lines of cocaine. The first two calls are to friends who he has not seen in quite some time. Neither is available to meet with him. The third call is to an erotic hotline, but as he brings his hand to the fly of his pants, something happens and he loses interest. His final call is to his mother, a desperate attempt to have a personal connection with someone outside of his work.

In López's fourth scene, his boss calls him in to his office to offer him a promotion to global sales director. Though a promotion, López would have to dedicate twenty-four hours a day to the company. When he asks who would be offered the job in the event he declined the offer, his boss says: "Tenemos a otra persona en mente. Concretamente, habíamos pensado en Muñoz. Su trabajo en China es excelente. Ha conseguido mucho, viniendo desde tan abajo. Le agradecemos a usted que nos lo recomendara" (We've actually got someone else in mind. Muñoz. His work in China has been excellent. Considering where he's come from, he's worked his way up and achieved a great deal. We're very grateful to you for recommending him) (*AP*, 90). The possibility of Muñoz being his boss causes López to accept on the spot. He does so in a repetition of the line he gave to Muñoz: "No. No hay nada que pensar. Acepto el puesto. Es la oportunidad de mi vida. Si la dejo pasar, me arrepentiré siempre" (No. There's nothing to think about. I accept your offer. It's the opportunity of a lifetime. If I let this pass me by, I'd always regret it) (*AP*, 90). The offer that cannot be refused seems to be karma coming full circle for López. In his final individual scene, López is in the Cairo airport waiting for his flight back to Madrid, which is delayed two hours. He ends up talking to a stranger who questions him on his life goals. López explains his life goal:

> Vivir sin trabajar. Como un rey. Sí. Como un rey. Voy a tener una casa junto al mar y dedicarme a la pesca.
>
> . . .
>
> Y siempre acompañado. Siempre. Siempre acompañado de una mujer con los ojos verdes. (*AP*, 26–27)

> I want to live without having to work. Like a king. Yeah. Like a king. I'm going to have a house by the sea and spend my time fishing.
>
> . . .
>
> But I'll always be in the company of someone. Always. Always in the company of a beautiful woman with green eyes.

Considering how dedicated López is to his corporate job, it is striking that his deepest desire is to be retired and accompanied by a woman in a place of tranquility. According to his calculations, he will be able to retire at fifty-nine, but at present he is only twenty-eight. He has resigned himself to the solitary demands of his job all in hopes of one day having that house by the sea and a beautiful woman by his side.

The story of Emma and Carlos follows the couple through their relationship before embarking on the trip to Egypt. In their first scene, Emma explains her tardiness for her date with Carlos by stating, "eso me pasa por divorciarme de mi despertador" (it's all because I divorced my alarm clock) (*AP*, 31). The function of her ex-husband was reduced to an alarm clock that also gave her sexual pleasure. This focus on sexual pleasure manifests in scene 2 when Carlos experiences erectile dysfunction in bed with Emma. When confronted with the embarrassment and shame, Carlos feels it necessary to explain his theory for why he cannot perform:

> CARLOS: Mi teoría es que eso me pasa por miedo. Por miedo a que eso me pase. Mi cuerpo nota el miedo que tengo de que eso me pase y provoca que me pase.
> EMMA: Eso es absurdo.
> CARLOS: O quizá es que mi cuerpo tiene miedo de que lo haga demasiado bien, que tenga la erección más impresionante de la historia de la humanidad, y entonces me ataca preventivamente para evitar que la especie evolucione tan deprisa, y es por eso que no puedo.

(*Emma mira fijamente a Carlos durante unos segundos. Rompe el silencio con sus carcajadas.*) (*AP*, 46)

> CARLOS. I think it's because I'm nervous. I'm afraid I won't be able to get it up. My body knows that and so it stops me from having one.
> EMMA. That's ridiculous.
> CARLOS. Or maybe my body's afraid of me being too good, that I'll have the most impressive erection in the history of mankind, and so it carries out a preventive attack to avoid the species evolving too quickly. Maybe that's why I can't get hard.

(*Emma stares at Carlos for a few seconds then breaks the silence with shrieks of laughter.*)

This excerpt is the only direct reference to the play's title, making it an interesting point of analysis. Carlos's two theories present very different logics. In the first, Carlos is trapped within a self-fulfilling prophecy in which his fear of not being able to perform prevents him from performing. In the second, he claims his body is attacking his erection because it could be the best ever known to man. This theory allows him to compensate for his lack of performance by promoting the abstract and untested claim that his erection is too impressive for the world to experience. In addition, the body's preventive attack on Carlos's erection allows him to maintain a posture of phallic superiority. Deep down, however, he knows that his lack of performance is an affront to his masculinity.

Carlos's fear manifests in anxiety attacks that restrict his breathing. At the end of the erectile dysfunction scene, he begins to have difficulty breathing and is in need of medicine:

EMMA. ¿Qué te pasa ahora?
CARLOS. (*Respirando cada vez más fuerte.*) Nada. No me pasa nada.

(*Carlos toma unas pastillas.*)

EMMA. ¿Por qué tomas tantas pastillas?
CARLOS. Son para dormir.
EMMA. ¿Tienes problemas para dormir?
CARLOS. No. Es que me gusta mucho dormir. Dormir profundamente y no enterarme de nada. Como si el mundo no existiera. (*AP*, 47)

EMMA. Now, what's the matter?
CARLOS. (*Breathing more and more heavily.*) Nothing. I'm fine.

(*Carlos takes some pills.*)

EMMA. What are all those pills for?
CARLOS. They're to help me sleep.
EMMA. Do you have problems sleeping?
CARLOS. No. It's just that I really like to sleep. I like to sleep so deeply that I'm not aware of anything around me. As if the world didn't exist.

Carlos's breathing becomes a signal of anxiety throughout the play, a fear that his relationship is on the verge of ending. His desire to sleep deeply hints at suicide, to be out of this world, able to sleep forever.

Carlos's fear is well grounded because in scene 3 we observe Emma with another man smoking marijuana. This man wants her to leave Carlos to be with him. She wants the man to swear that he will never abandon her. His response is telling:

HOMBRE: No voy a jurar. No sobre el futuro.
EMMA: ¿Por qué?
HOMBRE: Para que veas que no quiero engañarte. Sé lo que siento ahora, pero para mí ese tal "futuro" es un desconocido. Sólo sé una cosa: ahora, en este preciso momento, te adoro y quiero vivir contigo. (*AP*, 69)

MAN: I'm not going to swear anything. Not when it comes to the future.
EMMA: Why?
MAN: Because I don't want to lie to you. I know what I feel now, but for me, this so-called "future" is an unknown. I only know one thing: now, at this precise moment, I adore you and I want to spend my life with you.

Emma's insistence on fidelity is ironic as she is cheating on Carlos with this unnamed man. His inability to subscribe to Emma's concept of temporal fidelity, which is based in the future, as opposed to his, which is grounded in the present, leads her to leave him. Some days later, Carlos asks Emma about her ostensible outing with a friend at the film archive to see a classic film:

CARLOS. «Gilda», ¿verdad?
EMMA. Sí. Ya iba siendo hora de que la Viera . . .
CARLOS. Pues sí. Ya iba siendo hora. Está muy bien Humphrey Bogart en esa película, ¿verdad?
EMMA. Sí. Excelente. El mejor trabajo de su vida, diría yo.
CARLOS. Sin duda.

(*Silencio. Empieza a respirar fuerte, con dificultad.*) (*AP*, 81)

CARLOS. *Gilda*, that's right, isn't it?
EMMA. Yeah. You should see it.
CARLOS. Yeah, I should, while it's still on. I hear Humphrey Bogart's great in that film. Is that right?
EMMA. Yes, he's amazing. It's the best film he's done. Well, I think so anyway.
CARLOS. Without a doubt.

(*Silence. Carlos starts breathing loudly and with difficulty.*)

Carlos's fear is confirmed in this conversation as he traps Emma. *Gilda* is a 1946 American film starring Rita Hayworth, Glenn Ford, and George Macready; Humphrey Bogart does not appear in this film at all. Catching Emma in the lie sets off his anxiety attack.

In their final scene, Emma and Carlos are packing for Egypt and discuss how this trip will give them both the ability to escape. The desire for both of them to leave their relationship bubbles as a subtext, demonstrated in their final lines:

CARLOS: Me encanta volar, ¿te lo he dicho alguna vez?
EMMA: Sólo hay una pega . . .
CARLOS: Surcar las nubes, como un pájaro . . .
EMMA: Que se acaba tan pronto.
CARLOS: Hasta los pájaros tienen que aterrizar.
EMMA: Bueno, mejor no pensar en el final . . .
CARLOS: Sí.
EMMA: . . . cuando todavía no nos hemos ido.
CARLOS: Mejor.
EMMA: Mejor no pensar en el regreso.
CARLOS: Mejor. Sí. Mejor. (*AP*, 20)

CARLOS: I love flying. Have I ever told you that?
EMMA: There's only one downside . . .

CARLOS: Coming down through the clouds, just like a bird . . .
EMMA: It's all over so soon.
CARLOS: Even birds have to land.
EMMA: Well, it's best not to think about the end . . .
CARLOS: Yeah.
EMMA: . . . when we haven't even left yet.
CARLOS: Yeah, you're right.
EMMA: Best not to think about coming home.
CARLOS: Yeah, you're right, best not to.

To acknowledge the return to Madrid now not only preventively ends their vacation but also ends their ability to escape from the problems of their relationship.

The final character, Rachid, is also trying to escape from problems, but his are more financial in nature. Rachid and his wife are being evicted from their Madrid apartment because the rent has not been paid in a year. Rachid initially cited the death of his son as the cause of his debilitation, but the landlady is fed up with excuses.

CASERA. No vas a conseguir que me conmueva, Rachid. Hablas muy bien español. Y tienes suerte de tener papeles. No te costará conseguir trabajo.
RACHID. Era más fácil antes, sin papeles. ¿Quién quiere trabajadores si puede tener esclavos? (*AP*, 42)

LANDLADY: You're not going to win me over with that sob story, Rachid. You speak very good Spanish. And you're lucky enough to have a visa. It won't be hard to find work.
RACHID: It was easier before, without a visa. Who wants workers if they can have slaves?

The landlady presumptuously claims that Rachid's legal status will help him escape from debt, but legality seems to create a different kind of bondage. He now has to compete with undocumented migrants who are willing to accept lower wages that he cannot legally accept.

His inability to find work despite legal status creates a conundrum in which Rachid must revert to clandestine work to survive. In his second scene, Rachid makes phone calls for a deaf–mute man. In between calls, Rachid calls around looking for employment. His last call is to a Narcotraficante (Drug Trafficker) whom he will meet at a call shop. That evening, Rachid and his wife discuss how they can overcome the eviction notice. In scene 4, Rachid meets with his doctor, who prescribes him pills for a heart condition and gives him a note with advice on how to maintain a healthy heart. A déjà vu moment occurs when Rachid asks his doctor whether he is allowed to fly:

RACHID. ¿Puedo montar en avión?
MÉDICO. ¿En avión? Ni se le ocurra. Es muy arriesgado. Lo demás me lo podrá discutir si quiere, pero viajar en avión no es necesario. Peligro de muerte.
RACHID. Al final todos nos morimos. Incluso los médicos.
MÉDICO. Viajar en avión . . . Es algo que puede evitar perfectamente. ¿Para qué querría usted jugarse la vida?
RACHID. ¿Jugarme la vida? No es tan grave. Es lo que hago todos los días. (*AP*, 80)

RACHID. Can I fly?
DOCTOR. Fly? Don't even think about it. It's extremely risky. Others might disagree, but traveling by plane is unnecessary. You'd be toying with death.
RACHID. We all die in the end. Even doctors.
DOCTOR. Flying . . . is something that can easily be avoided. Why would you want to risk your life?
RACHID. Risk my life? That's no big deal. It's what I do every day.

Rachid's heart condition, already exacerbated by the stress of unemployment and the eviction, would surely be fatal in the compressed space of an airplane. Risk, however, is part of Rachid's life and identity as a North African in Spain. His legal status gives him rights, but his race and ethnicity simultaneously erase them.

This risk grows exponentially in Rachid's final scene in which he speaks to Narcotraficante in person regarding the mission to traffic drugs between Spain and Egypt. Narcotraficante explains that it is actually less risky to smuggle merchandise through airports as surveillance has weakened due to increased trafficking via alternative paths. When Rachid asks whether Spaniards do this type of work, Narcotraficante slyly responds:

NARCOTRAFICANTE: Muy pocos. No hay gente tan desesperada. Sólo alguien que no tiene a dónde agarrarse se atreve. Por eso venimos al locutorio a buscaros. Si los europeos quieren jugar al peligro prefieren ir al parque de atracciones. O ponerse con eso que tú les vas a llevar.
RACHID: Arriesgo vida para que ellos se diviertan. (*AP*, 91)

DRUG TRAFFICKER: Very few of them. People aren't that desperate. Only someone with nothing left to hold onto would take the risk. That's why we come to the internet café to look for you. If Europeans want a taste of danger, they prefer to go to a theme park. Or take what you're going to bring them.
RACHID: I risk my life just so they have good time.

The sad reality of the drug trade suddenly becomes clear: impoverished migrants (documented or not) are the only ones willing to do the work that provides the illicit market for Spaniards. Rachid will simply serve as a mule to fuel the various addictions that we see in the other characters: cocaine, marijuana, prescription pills, and so forth. Knowing the value of his journey, Rachid negotiates to be paid €8,000 instead of €4,000, because as he states: "Necesito ese dinero. Lo necesito de verdad. Y lo necesitará mi hijo" (I need this money. I really need it. My son needs it) (*AP*, 93). This emotional end to Rachid's story line is compounded by the nonlinear structure of the play, because as the play progresses, the spectator gains more respect for Rachid as they learn his motivations and struggles.

Unfortunately, by the time the affective tie to Rachid is made, his death has been belabored through the discussions that occur on the plane. This is because Rachid's story line scenes are presented in chronological order (1, 2, 3, 4, 5), whereas the other four individual story lines start right before the flight and then flash back in time (5, 1, 2, 3, 4). This distinction is crucial for understating how Rachid is perceived. The play starts with Plane scene 1 with an offstage enunciation of death, "Está muerto" (He is dead) (*AP*, 17). Starting the play in this way triggers a series of questions: Who is dead and how did he or she die? Few answers are divulged in the first plane scene, as we are only able to observe Carlos telling the rest of the cabin that neither the captain nor anyone else should know what happened. Claudia, the flight attendant, then covers the body of a man (who we later learn is Rachid) and at the start of the second plane scene says: "Ya está. Nadie más de la tripulación pasará por aquí hasta que aterricemos. Los de clase turista no tienen acceso a esta zona. Tenemos suerte de ser pocos" (It's settled. No other crew member will pass through here until we land. Economy class passengers do not have access to this area. We are lucky to be so few) (*AP*, 29). This decision implicates the five living people in the first-class cabin in the death of the man.

In trying to come up with a solution to the hysteria, they discuss a plan:

CLAUDIA. Deberíamos hablar. Que cada uno cuente lo que hizo y lo que vio. Y decidir qué contarle a la policía cuando aterricemos en Madrid.
EMMA. ¿De cuánto tiempo disponemos?
CLAUDIA. Sólo 45 minutos.
EMMA. Es más de lo que esperaba. Pensé que estábamos a punto de llegar.
LÓPEZ. Yo también. Todo ha sucedido tan rápido . . .
CARLOS. Tampoco nos sobra el tiempo. Hablemos.
CLAUDIA. Debemos dar sólo una versión. Una versión única. Es la mejor manera de prevenir problemas.
LÓPEZ. Hablemos. Nos pondremos de acuerdo todos y contaremos siempre la misma historia.
CARLOS. De acuerdo. Manos a la obra. ¿Cuál será la verdad? (*AP*, 30)

CLAUDIA. We should talk. Each of us should tell what they did and what they saw. And decide what to tell the police when we land in Madrid.
EMMA. How much time do we have left?
CLAUDIA. Only forty-five minutes.
EMMA. It's more than I expected. I thought we were about to arrive.
LÓPEZ. Me too. Everything has happened so quickly . . .
CARLOS. We do not have too much time. Let's talk.
CLAUDIA. We should give only one version. A single version. It's the best way to prevent problems.
LÓPEZ. Let's talk. We will all agree and will always tell the same story.
CARLOS. Ok. Let's get to it. What will be the truth?

This rapid-fire discussion solidifies one truth: a man is dead and everyone present is responsible. We still do not understand why, however. Claudia, as a flight attendant, knows the procedure of what will happen once the plane lands. Police will likely interview all five of them to learn how the man died. It is interesting to note that the only character absent from this discussion is Sonia, the youngest character. At the beginning of this scene, she screams: "¡Quiero irme! Yo no tengo nada que ver con esto. No quiero tener nada que ver con ustedes. No quiero que me encuentren al lado de un muerto cuando aterrice el avión" (I want to leave! I have nothing to do with this. I don't want anything to do with you all. I don't want them to find me next to a dead man when we land) (*AP*, 29). Carlos rebukes and silences her by retorting: "Tú te quedas. Nos quedamos todos. Y tú sí tienes que ver con esto. Si no, ¿por qué tendrías tantas ganas de largarte? . . . Ella empezó todo esto. Si no fuera por ella, seguiríamos volando tranquilamente" (You stay. We all stay. And yes, you have something to do with this. If not, why would you have such a desire to flee? . . . She started all this. If not for her, we would still be flying quietly) (*AP*, 29). Knowing that Sonia is prone to anxiety attacks, often triggered by men that make her feel vulnerable, it is understandable that she would be on the verge of an attack given the stress of the situation.

In the third plane scene, we observe that many of the passengers were nervous about Rachid's presence in first class because he was loud and rude to Claudia regarding the airline's silverware. Rachid stated that he wanted a better knife because the one he had did not cut the meat well. As Claudia recalls: "Yo le dije que no teníamos otros. Que eran las normas. Que desde lo del 11 de septiembre estaban totalmente prohibidos los cubiertos afilados. Que si quería le cambiaba la carne por otra. Y fue entonces cuando sacó la navaja" (I told him we didn't have any other cutlery. That it was the rules. That sharp knives have been banned since 9/11, and that if he wanted, I could change the meat for another kind. And that's when he pulled out the knife) (*AP*, 44). Pulling out a knife on board a plane only exacerbated rising anxieties about Rachid's presence.

The irony of this scene is its milieu: the first-class cabin of an airplane. Although we have no information about the airline, first-class cabins are generally known for their higher level of service with regard to the in-flight dining experience. Such a privileged space, however, is still bound by international aviation law banning sharp knives post–September 11th. The scene ends with Claudia's suspenseful description, but given that the text provides no signs of aggression on Rachid's part, in fact, in Plane scene 5, Claudia describes Rachid calmly enjoying his meal. When Claudia's reaction is discussed, she explains: "Tuve que hacerlo. Le dije que estaba prohibido llevar una navaja en el avión. Y le grité porque no estaba segura de que me entendiera" (I had to do it. I told him that carrying knives on the flight was prohibited. And I shouted because I wasn't sure he understood me) (*AP*, 59). Her yelling is not out of anger or disbelief, but rather out of prejudice, which is highlighted by Carlos, who affirms that Rachid spoke Spanish very well (spectators already know that from Rachid's story line).

Not knowing his name, the passengers debate whether to call him "the terrorist" or "the alleged terrorist" when Carlos asks López to repeat to everyone what he said before they attacked Rachid:

> Le dije que era un moro con una navaja. Un puto moro con una navaja. (*Irónico, a Carlos.*) ¿Está mejor así? Le dije que cuántas posibilidades habría de que un moro con una navaja, en un avión con destino a un país occidental, no fuera un terrorista. ¿Cuántas posibilidades? Una entre un millón, ¿no? Eso le dije. Fue el calor del momento. (*AP*, 61)
>
> I said that he was a Paki with a knife. A fucking Paki with a knife. (*Sarcastically, to Carlos.*) Is that better now? I said to him: "What are the chances of there being a Paki with a knife on a flight from a Middle Eastern country and him not being a terrorist? What are the chances of that? One in a million, right?" That's what I said. In the heat of the moment.

The rhetoric espoused here, presented in a pseudostatistical manner, is racist, as Sonia is quick to blurt out, but López's retort gets to the root of the issue: "Mírame a los ojos y dime que no pensabas lo mismo cuando estabas ahí temblando con tu puto ataque de ansiedad" (Look me in the eye and tell me that you weren't thinking the same when you were there trembling with your fucking anxiety attack) (*AP*, 61). The fourth plane scene serves to demonstrate each character's implicit bias toward Middle Eastern men.

In Plane scene 5, the passengers recount the attack on Rachid. First, Carlos snuck up on him to grab the knife and throw it on the ground. When Rachid stands up, enraged that he couldn't finish his meal, Carlos punched him down to the ground. López then kicked Rachid several times in the stomach as he lay on the ground. The stress of the situation causes Rachid to have a heart attack and die. As the men narrate to the group, Sonia searches Rachid's cadaver for anything that might help the group absolve itself. She finds the doctor's note that we see in Rachid's fifth scene. Knowing Rachid's heart condition, the group is able to exculpate itself:

> EMMA. (*A Claudia.*) Me alegro de que todo se solucionara. Sabía que éramos inocentes.
> CLAUDIA. Yo también. Lo que nunca entenderé es lo que había en la cabeza de ese hombre para subirse a un avión en esas condiciones.
> EMMA. Ya se sabe. No está bien que yo lo diga estando él de cuerpo presente, pero hay gente que no sabe cuidarse. Hay gente que no valora su cuerpo y no sabe lo que es prevenir. (*AP*, 95)

> EMMA. (*To Claudia.*) I'm so glad we've resolved all this. I knew we were innocent.
> CLAUDIA. Me too. The thing I'll never understand is what that man was thinking, getting on a plane in that condition.
> EMMA. Well, now we know. It's not very nice of me to say this in his presence, but some people just don't know how to look after themselves. Some people don't value their own bodies and don't understand the importance of prevention.

Only the spectators are privy to Rachid's deadly secret: he risked his life to save and provide for his family. Claudia's rhetorical statement could be posed to any character: What is going on in their head to take this flight? The escapism of air travel, a non-migratory movement, allows the Spanish characters to take a break from the stress of their lives that leads each of them to drugs (another form of escapism). Similarly, Emma's two statements are just as problematic. Is the group actually innocent as they attacked Rachid, thereby provoking his heart attack? Their ability to create a group alibi is a result of their small numbers and everyone's individual involvement in the death. Had this occurred in economy class, there is a much lower probability that a cover-up could have been fabricated. The importance of prevention she references in her second statement is multifaceted. In terms of health, the characters are not truly taking care of themselves given the constant reference to stress and drug use. However, I think the underlying message pertains to efforts to stave off Otherness within Spain. Rachid's inability to look after himself and his family (lack of income and shelter) constitutes justification for his removal from the Spanish national body as he is unable to prevent his own poverty and has no means from which to escape it, other than illegal activity.

The play's final line captures the nefarious nature of what happened in the first-class cabin: "Capitán. Debo informarle de una incidencia que ha afectado a uno de los pasajeros. La situación es muy grave. Pero está bajo control" (Captain, I must inform you, there's been an incident that has affected one of our passengers. The situation is very serious. But it's under control) (*AP*, 98). By not notifying the captain when the incident first occurred, Claudia is complicit in the death of Rachid. To end by stating that the situation is under control, symbolically represents the erasure of Rachid, the metonymy of a problematic people. Philosopher Lewis Gordon defines "problematic people," proposing, "They cease to be people who might face, signify, or be associated with a set of problems: they *become* those problems."[34] Rachid, and other North African migrants, by no choice of their own, have *become* the issues that Spain projects upon them. The threat of terrorism portrayed in this play cultivates a prophylactic culture, which thereby justifies the use of the preventive attacks. This same justification exists in the Reconquista, during which Christian kingdoms justified attacking the Muslim south as a way to prevent its expansion and take back the peninsula.

Undying Antagonism

The antagonistic dynamic between Spain and North Africa is centuries old, persisting through the reimagining of the Reconquista in which Spaniards again must resist the "invasion" of the nation by the Moors, now understood to be immigrants from Morocco and other North African nations. Considering the almost mythological threat that North African immigrants allegedly pose to Spanish culture and society, their theatrical representation is not as bleak as might be expected. Although none of the plays explored in this chapter have the idyllic endings sometimes seen in the portrayal of Latin American migrants, neither do they have the tragic endings seen in the portrayals of sub-Saharan African immigrants. Two distinct themes are present in the representation of North African immigrants: identity negotiation and Islamophobia as a result of terrorism. Both require North African characters to prove their ability to integrate into Spanish society to be accepted. In all cases, however, they are set up to fail: acceptance and integration are not possible because they represent the eternal enemy to the Spanish state, the Moor. Flesler claims, "The hierarchy of acceptance corresponds, more or less, to a scheme in which Europeans, both from EU countries and not, are at the top of the list, followed by Latin Americans, then sub-Saharan Africans, with North Africans at the bottom."[35] The theatrical representation of North Africans does not support this claim, however, because plays concerning this group end in ways that cause the reader/spectator to reflect on the autochthonous reactions to and treatment of this migrant group. It is the Spanish characters' bellicose response to these migrants that drives the plays to their fatalistic and necropolitical denouements, but their militaristic stance is satirically displayed so as to critique its usefulness.

As the erroneous and anachronistic reincarnation of the Moor, a figure that embodies the Spanish fight for national identity, North African migrants must battle centuries of institutionalized racism and simultaneously prove that they come in peace. The growing size of this migrant community simply incites and entrenches Maurophobia as if the "invasion" of 711 were slowly coming to fruition again. However, whereas North Africans have become a place-holder for the mythical enemy—the Moor who wishes to reclaim the land that was taken from him—chapter 3 will demonstrate that sub-Saharan Africans have come to be viewed as a more clear and present danger, a fear that they will dismantle the power of whiteness as retribution for Spanish colonialism and slavery.

Chapter 3

✦

En Route to Death

Spanish Necropolitical Theater and the Precarity of Black Immigration

In 1993, the first play to explicitly portray the immigration of sub-Saharan Africans, Ignacio del Moral's *La mirada del hombre oscuro*, debuted in Madrid. This play established a narrative motif in which the journey of black African migrants culminates in their death. This tragic end is present in the fourteen other plays that have been written between 1991 and 2016, in which the black African (predominately male) body is displayed as one that is desperate, poor, and ultimately undeserving of living in Spain. The plays I will analyze in this chapter are *La mirada del hombre oscuro* (*LMHO*) by Ignacio del Moral, *La falsa muerte de Jaro el Negro* (*LFMJN*) by Fernando Martín Iniesta, and *Friday* by Irma Correa.[1] In these plays, the representation of the death of the black migrant functions as a way to mitigate autochthonous Spanish feelings of insecurity or even inferiority. In this chapter, I explore the necropolitics of black immigration to answer the following questions: Why is the depiction of their death necessary to discuss their migration? What does death symbolize regarding the integration of Africans into Spanish society? How does the death of the migrant implicate the autochthonous Spanish protagonists or spectators, or both? How does this correlate with Spain's overall attitude toward Africans? By answering these questions, I will demonstrate that these three plays highlight not only the precarity of the border (land/sea/air) that the migrants cross but also the precarity of their bodies as agents of Otherness inhabiting the Spanish national stage in both figurative and literal terms.

The presence of sub-Saharan Africans in the Spanish national imaginary dates back to the fifteenth century when the transatlantic slave trade and colonialism in Latin America and Africa established cross-cultural bonds that exist even today.[2] Their presence in Spain was sparse, however, until the early 1990s when Spain's economic success and open immigration policy created an amenable environment for migrants. As a result of this new wave of migration, however, it was common to see headlines about the "drama" of immigration, referring to the risky, and often deadly, manner in which sub-Saharan African migrants attempted to enter Spain. This "drama" was attracting international attention at a time when Spain was entering the global spotlight for its positive contributions (e.g., hosting the 1992 Summer Olympic Games in Barcelona and the 1992 World Fair in Seville).[3] It is fitting, then, that Spanish playwrights wished to capture this drama in their works because as Marco Kunz astutely establishes in his chapter on immigration dramas, "El arte teatral establece un contacto inmediato con su público y es, por consiguiente, un medio que se presta por excelencia para reaccionar ante problemas actuales, con la intención de provocar discusiones y contribuir así al debate político" (Theater establishes an immediate contact with its audience and consequently is a medium that lends itself par excellence to reacting to social problems with the intention of provoking discussions, thereby contributing to political debate).[4] The plays discussed in this chapter are all inspired by news stories concerning the death of sub-Saharan African migrants en route to or already living in Spain. In this way, these plays engage directly with social and political debates regarding immigration and Spain's relationship with Africa.

Spain's contemporary history with Africa is shaped by its presence in Morocco, Western Sahara, and Equatorial Guinea, all of which cut formal colonial ties with Spain by the end of the Franco regime. Bernabé López explains that the independence of these former colonies, unlike in France and England, did not result in immediate migratory flows toward the metropole.[5] In Spain, this process would occur decades later and have more to do with geographic proximity than colonial ties, as Morocco and Algeria provide the majority of African immigrants into Spain. However, Spain's relationship with sub-Saharan Africa is notably distinct from that with North Africa, as described in chapter 2. In addition to having distinct colonial histories, the racial politics of the two groups are discoursed in vastly different ways, thus necessitating their separation.

Sub-Saharan Africans' migration into Spain can be mapped to three main areas: the coasts of Andalucía and Murcia, the Spanish enclaves of Melilla and Ceuta, and the Canary Islands. These migrants most commonly come from Senegal, The Gambia, Nigeria, and Equatorial Guinea, although there are some from the rest of the region as well. The arrival points are predominately coastal, such that the main method of migration is through the use of *pateras* and *cayucos*. If the use of such boats in the open seas were not precarious enough, they are often overloaded with people, not allowing space for food and important supplies. The close quarters, careless abandon of sanitary and safety conditions, and "commodity-like" nature of the transport all bear an uncanny resemblance to the Middle Passage from the days of the transatlantic slave trade, but today this migration is predominately voluntary and paid. The result is the death of many in the boats along the way, not to mention those who drown when the sea overcomes the crafts they occupy.

Another possible method of entry is to scale the border walls of Ceuta and Melilla. These walls were constructed in the late 1990s and later reinforced over the next two decades in response to the sharp rise in immigration. During these reinforcements, a series of obstacles were added to make the crossing more difficult. Journalist Isabella Alexander observes: "Because scaling the fences around the Spanish enclaves of Ceuta and Melilla requires no smuggling fees, no purchasing of false documents, no life jackets or iron cages, it is the route taken by the most desperate. And because, in the forest camps of northern Morocco, the most desperate are the majority, it is the route taken by nearly all."[6] Although there is a clear economic advantage to this route, Alexander's research indicates that the probability of scaling the wall is about 1 for every 500 that attempt it on any given day. This low success rate has led to the proliferation of *harragas* in northern Morocco. This term is derived from "'Hrig,' the Moroccan Arabic term for 'illegal immigration,' [which] translates to 'burning.'"[7] It signifies the literal burning of one's identification papers to evade repatriation if arrested by European authorities, but it also signifies the symbolic burning of one's past in hopes of a better future abroad.

This population, which is impossible to repatriate according to legal protocol as they have destroyed their documents, now forms large camps in the Moroccan mountains outside of the walled cities of Ceuta and Melilla. For example, when the Gourougou camp (located in the mountains between Melilla and the Moroccan city of Nador) was raided by Moroccan forces in 2014, makeshift dwellings were destroyed and camp residents were rounded up and shipped to an immigration detention center in the south of the country. Such raids have become more frequent in the last several years as the Moroccan government aims to stop the flow of migrants into the Spanish enclaves, thus serving as an accomplice to Spain's maintenance of "Fortress Europe." These camps can be viewed as the inverse of the Maroon communities in the Caribbean in which runaway black slaves formed communities in the mountains and forests outside of cities. This inversion proposes that today freedom exists within the walls of whiteness, a concept with dangerous implications considering that many of Africa's problems derive from European interventions on the continent.

Given Spain's proximity to Africa, one must ask why there are not more Africans in Spain today. The answer can be found in the "ethnic filter" that existed within Spain's original immigration policy, the *Ley Orgánica sobre los derechos y libertades de los extranjeros en España* enacted in 1985. In an effort to rectify its colonial wrongs, a list of nationalities was given preferential treatment: Ibero-Americans, Portuguese, Filipinos, Andorrans, Equatoguineans, Sephardim, and those from the city of Gibraltar.[8] Sub-Saharan Africans, with the exception of those from Equatorial Guinea (Spain's sole former colony in the region), could not get access to visas and work permits, thus sparking the dangerous, clandestine migration that has led to the death of thousands of men, women, and children who have attempted to cross the

Mediterranean Sea to reach the peninsula or the Atlantic to reach the Canary Islands, or to scale the border walls to reach Ceuta and Melilla. Sources estimate that around thirty thousand sub-Saharan Africans are in Algeria and Morocco hoping to arrive in Spain, which pales in comparison, for example, with the more than one million Latin Americans that entered Spain between 2000 and 2004.[9] The barrage of media imagery of border crossers, *pateras*, and drowned bodies has falsely created a perception of an "invasion" from Africa, even though sub-Saharan Africans make up a very small percentage of immigrants (12.4 percent in 2016).

What ultimately separates the portrayal of this group in comparison with the others discussed in this book thus far is its degree of blackness. As Antumi Toasije proclaims, "The anomalous concentration of information regarding nonregular immigration as a kind of new crime on television, press, and radio shows the fact that Europe in general and Spain in particular, because of racist myths forged in slavery and colonial eras, fear African migration."[10] Furthermore, given that the migration of sub-Saharan migrants has been consistently majority male (65 percent) for the last decade, the phobogenic perception of the black male body only compounds the societal fear of such immigration. Ignacio del Moral's *La mirada del hombre oscuro*, Fernando Martín Iniesta's *La falsa muerte de Jaro el Negro*, and Irma Correa's *Friday* encapsulate the degree to which death is used as a didactical instrument for the spectator, ultimately promoting a national imaginary in which black people cannot survive, let alone thrive.

Death by Toxic Masculinity in *La mirada del hombre oscuro*

It is through a portrayal of antagonistic masculinities that Ignacio del Moral's 1991 play *La mirada del hombre oscuro* (*Dark Man's Gaze*) theatrically depicts the then-new phenomenon of African migration to Spain via *pateras*. The play debuted January 8, 1993, at the Teatro Olimpia in Madrid. It also was the winner of the 1991 Premio de Teatro de la Sociedad General de Autores de España. In 1996, the play was adapted by director Imanol Uribe into the film *Bwana*, which was Spain's entry that year for Best Foreign Film at the Oscars. Although the film has been studied much more than the play, del Moral's work is notable for establishing the theatrical canon from which other playwrights have since departed.

The play is the story of Ombasi, an African migrant who washes up on Spanish shores with a companion who has died. On this same beach, there is a Spanish family fishing for clams. Upon encountering the family, Ombasi is unable to communicate in Spanish, knowing only one phrase: "¡Viva España!, ¡Butragueño!"[11] As he approaches the family, who thinks he wants to rob them, El Padre empties his pockets to give Ombasi all he has. In the process, he misplaces the spark plug to the car, which he had removed to prevent someone from being able to steal the car while they combed the beach for clams. As a result of losing the spark plug, the family is stranded on the beach and thus forced to interact with Ombasi to survive the night, since he was able to start a fire to keep himself warm. The next morning, El Padre is able to find the spark plug, allowing them to leave the beach. Ombasi wishes to go with them but is aggressively rejected by the patriarch, leading to a fight in which the latter gets sand in his eye, causing him to lose sight. Before the fight worsens, a Civil Guard helicopter arrives to "save" the family. Ombasi, mostly unscathed, is apprehended by the authorities, sent to a detention center in Madrid, and deported soon after. He then makes the journey a second time, arriving in Madrid only to die homeless and sick during the cold winter. He collapses into a dirty puddle in the Madrid metro and drowns as passengers walk past him.

The play is a reflection of the all too common news reports (even today) of black bodies washing up on the Spanish coast. As del Moral himself states in the prologue to the play:

> El detonante a que aludo fue una foto de prensa que, con esa descarnada impudicia que a menudo nos embota, pero que de cuando en cuando, tiene la virtud de provocar un dolor profundo en la conciencia, mostraba los cadáveres de dos infortunados emigrantes africanos que, tratando de llegar a nuestras costas, se habían ahogado, siendo las olas las encargadas de cumplir, siquiera póstumamente, su deseo de llegar a la dorada Europa. (*LMHO*, 11)
>
> The trigger I allude to was a moving photo in a newspaper that, with that brutal immodesty that often weakens us, but that every so often has the power to provoke deep pain in our conscience, showed the bodies of two unfortunate African emigrants, who had drowned trying to reach our coast, such that the waves were entrusted with fulfilling, albeit posthumously, their desire to reach Golden Europe.

The author's language elucidates an understanding of the necropolitics at play in del Moral's work. There is a clear relationship between the press and the nation's emotional response. The migrants' desire to reach Europe's shores can only be fulfilled by Mother Nature, as Europe would not accept them otherwise. Although nature is not personified in the play, it has a clear role in the plot development as weather steers the fates of Ombasi and the other protagonists. Death by drowning is a common occurrence for African migrants, thus explaining the fate of the play's two African characters, symbolizing their collective inability to inhabit Spain, or "Golden Europe," as del Moral calls it.

As *La mirada del hombre oscuro* was inspired by black death, its title and cast evoke dichotomies that foreshadow the tragic denouement. The title's reference to an *hombre oscuro* (dark man) can take on three possible meanings. The first puts emphasis on Ombasi's dark complexion as his defining ontological trait, insinuating that his otherness is entwined with his blackness. The second interpretation would be to understand the word *oscuro* as dark, sinister, and malevolent, which would imply that Ombasi's gaze is threatening to the Spanish nation's status quo. In addition, the preposition *del* indicates a possessive agency in which the plot privileges his gaze or narrative perspective. The play's plot is, however, more about the Spanish family's reaction to Ombasi than his reaction to them, thus creating a third interpretation of the title: the Spaniard as a dark figure for his or her ignorance and racism.

Within the cast, Ombasi is the only character with a proper name. This decision could convey the playwright's attempt to humanize Ombasi and privilege him as the play's central protagonist. The other five characters are named according to Ombasi's direct relationship with them: El Padre (Father), La Madre (Mother), El Niño (Boy), La Niña (Little Girl), and El Cadáver (The Body). The lack of proper names for the Spanish characters can be seen as a way to universalize or metonymize the family to represent Spain, such that the play's action depicts a microcosm of Spain's contemporary relationship with African migrants. There is also the distinction between the two African characters presented as a binary between life and death. Though companions along the journey and in the afterlife in the final scene, their interactions throughout the play all relate to death: burial, protection of the tomb, the foreshadowing of Ombasi's death, and finally Ombasi's entrance into the afterlife following his own death. This necrological plot line weaves death and blackness from beginning to end.

The play begins necrologically as La Niña screams, "¡Hay unos negros muertos, hay unos negros muertos!" (Dead black men! Dead black men!), after falling behind one of the sand dunes and landing at the bottom where Ombasi lays exhaustedly next to his dead compatriot.[12] The emphatic reference to race and death portends the play's ending when we learn of Ombasi's death in scene 14. The young girl's hysterical reaction permeates the entire family, evidenced by scene 3 when Ombasi speaks to the family for the first time, attempting to introduce himself:

> OMBASI. La niña se ha caído, pero no es nada. Tengo hambre. Me llamo Ombasi. (*Para hacerse entender, señala a la niña, se señala a sí mismo, hace gesto de comer.*)
> EL NIÑO. ¡Dice que se quiere comer a la niña! (*LMHO*, 23)

> OMBASI. The little girl fell, but it's not serious. I'm hungry. My name is Ombasi. (*To make himself understood, HE [OMBASI] points to the LITTLE GIRL, then to himself, then makes an eating gesture.*)
> BOY. He's saying he wants to eat her![13] (*DMG*, 5)

El Niño's horrified reaction is understandable given Ombasi's hand gestures, but it contradicts what spectators hear from Ombasi. This disconnect results from Ombasi's Spanish (except for "¡Viva España, Butragueño!," the one phrase he repeats to the family) being extradiegetic, serving solely to allow spectators to understand him and his thoughts. Within the diegetic world of the play, Ombasi speaks an African language that is unintelligible to the Spanish family, hence their incredulous reactions. While the family's lack of comprehension and the audience's omniscient knowledge add to the humor of the play, they also enable the rampant use of racist language as the Spanish family can speak about Ombasi without his understanding. It is the lack of comprehension via both language and prejudice that leads to a necropolitical end.

There are two narrative levels in this play: the real and the oneiric, both foreshadowing negative outlooks for Ombasi's migratory prospects. Spectators observe racism in the real world through a series of prejudicial statements made mainly by La Madre. In scene 3, for example, upon "losing" the spark plug, El Padre decides to ask Ombasi to help him find it. The father's use of body language indicates a car more so than a spark plug, which does not help Ombasi to understand. In response, La Madre states: "¿Lo ves? ¡Este no ha visto un coche en su vida!" (See? He's never seen a car in his life!) (*LMHO*, 30; *DMG*, 8). Later, when her daughter asks why Ombasi always repeats the same phrase in Spanish, she says, "Porque estas personas negras son muy incultas" (Because those black people are very uncivilized), which is ironic given the family's physically and verbally abusive interpersonal relationships (*LMHO*, 33; *DMG*, 10). These stereotypical views of black people are at their core, racist, but they serve to build a lexicon that facilitates what Etienne Balibar calls "prophylaxis," the use of exclusionary tactics to prevent racial and cultural mixing vis-à-vis immigration.[14]

The air of superiority she carries is quickly deflated in scene 6 when the family is stranded at the beach with no way to stay warm at night. Ombasi, having taken the lighter that El Padre throws away in his frenetic search for the spark plug, starts a fire behind one of the dunes. Realizing that they have no choice but to join him around the fire so as not to freeze during the night, La Madre yells at her husband:

> ¡Mira, Antonio, no me toques más las narices! ¡La niña va a coger una pulmonía y este negro tiene aquí un fuego que no sé ni cómo lo ha hecho, bueno, sí, claro que lo sé, lo ha hecho con tu dichoso mechero, porque me está pareciendo que este negro es más listo que tú, que lo único que has hecho ha sido tirar la bujía, así que eres tú mucho más caribe que él. (*LMHO*, 41)
>
> Look, Antonio, don't try me! This little girl's going to get pneumonia and this black man has a fire here that I don't even know how

> he's started. (*Pause.*) Well, yes, of course I know how, he did it with that infamous lighter of yours! It seems to me that this black man is smarter than you, seeing as the only thing you've done is throw away the spark plug, which makes you much more of a savage than him. (*DMG*, 13)

La Madre not only attacks her husband's capacity as a father but also his intelligence, survival skills, and common sense. The rhetorical juxtaposition to Ombasi's "savagery" initiates a rivalry of masculinity in which El Padre must demonstrate that he is a better man than Ombasi. As the plot unfolds, his attempts at imposing his "superior" masculinity fail and backfire. However, these failures only exacerbate the family's fear of Ombasi, transforming him into what Frantz Fanon calls the "'phobogenic' object, provoking anxiety."[15]

This anxiety is realized in scenes 7 and 8, during which La Madre and El Padre argue about falling asleep with Ombasi so near, as he may pose a risk to the entire family. El Padre believes there is nothing to fear and wishes to sleep, to which La Madre retorts, "Toda la familia en peligro y tú te duermes" (Your whole family is in danger and you're sleeping) (*LMHO*, 60; *DMG*, 22). After more arguing, La Madre falls asleep and dreams that Ombasi attempts to rape her. The stage directions that begin scene 8 state:

> *OMBASI, de repente abre los ojos y se queda mirando con fijeza a la mujer dormida. La mujer se despierta sobresaltada y le mira. Se miran un instante. OMBASI, a rastras, se acerca a ella. Cuando están juntos, él le levanta la falda. Ella le mira hacer, aterrorizada, pero sin oponer resistencia. OMBASI acaricia a la madre y besa sus muslos. Ella abre la boca en un grito que no llega a salir. Mira a su marido y le sacuda para despertarlo, en vano.*
>
> *Se hace un oscuro brevísimo y de nuevo están todos en su posición. La mujer se despierta sobresaltada, y mira a su alrededor. Mira a OMBASI, que duerme agitándose.*
>
> *La mujer suspira y mira a sus hijos, que duermen tranquilos. Se acerca a su marido, buscando protección. El hombre mascullа entre sueños. (LMHO, 62–63)*
>
> *OMBASI suddenly opens his eyes and stares at the sleeping woman. The WOMAN awakens, shaken, and looks at him. THEY look at each other for a moment. OMBASI, crawling, approaches her. When he reaches her, HE raises her skirt. SHE watches as he does so, terrified, but does not resist. OMBASI caresses her and kisses her thighs.*
>
> *MOTHER opens her mouth to a silent scream. She looks at her husband and shakes him in a vain attempt to wake him up.*

> *Short blackout. When the lights come up,* THEY *are back in their positions. The* WOMAN *awakens, shaken, and looks at her surroundings. She looks at* OMBASI, *who sleeps fitfully.* SHE *sighs and looks at her children sleeping tranquilly.* SHE *moves closer to her husband, seeking protection. (DMG, 23)*

The dream signals La Madre's fear of Ombasi, emblematic of the ingrained, latent Western fear of the black man as an ominous sexual predator, which would confirm autochthonous Spanish xenophobic anxieties about black African immigrants not simply stealing Spanish jobs but also Spanish women. It is worth noting that the unwanted sexual advance is sensual in nature rather than violent. This could be interpreted as a manifestation of the common Western view of the black man as an object of sexual desire. The oscillation between repugnance and desire in this dream exists because, as Camilla Stevens notes, "Se teme al negro por sus supuestos poderes sexuales" (The black man is feared for his supposed sexual powers).[16] This dynamic is demonstrated in the sensual nature of the dream, which connotes Ombasi's allure as well as the imminent danger of his Otherness. In search of refuge from the phobogenic agent of her dream, La Madre seeks the protection of her husband, who is asleep (both in the dream and in reality). The inability of El Padre to serve as a protector cements her unhappiness with her husband (which explodes in a later scene). This juncture in the text marks the point of no return for El Padre's masculinity, as he is no longer seen as a man in the eyes of his wife.

Meanwhile, in the oneiric realm, Ombasi receives warnings from El Cadáver (the ethereal presence of Ombasi's dead friend) regarding the Spanish family (and by extension, Spanish society), their racialized fear of African migrants, and its negative repercussions for Ombasi. In scene 8, Ombasi carries out an oneiric conversation with his friend, El Cadáver, who speaks candidly about the migratory process and the challenges that Ombasi will face. In response to Ombasi's thoughts that life in Spain will be better than the arduous journey, El Cadáver retorts:

> Aquí será peor. Aquí no nos quieren. Ni siquiera les interesamos para robarnos. Creen que venimos a quitarles lo suyo. Aunque nos conformemos con lo que ellos no quieren, es igual. Creen que les manchamos el aire pestilente que respiran. Ya has visto a estos. Se comportaban como si fueras a matarles. La mujer ha soñado que ibas a forzarla. (*LMHO*, 65)

> It'll be worse here. Here, they don't like us. Nor do they even care enough to rob us. They think we've come to take what is theirs. Even if we settle for what they don't want, it doesn't matter. They think we pollute the stinking air they breathe. You've seen these people. They acted like you were going to kill them. The woman dreamed you were going to rape her. (*DMG*, 24)

Since many sub-Saharan African migrants who take the maritime route come with little more than the clothes on their backs, they, unlike the African continent, whose natural riches have been pillaged by Western powers for centuries, are not even worth robbing. The reference to pollution is a powerful metaphor that appears in other immigration plays in which autochthonous characters view the immigrant as a contaminating force with the capacity to permanently destroy the Spanish atmosphere (i.e., society).[17] The black male migrant is not only a phobogenic pollutant for being the Other, but also for being black. The Spanish family's fear, albeit irrational, is an allegory for the autochthonous anxieties of Spain vis-à-vis immigration.

Spain's xenophobia portrayed in the play is ironic given its own citizens' history of emigration throughout the twentieth century. However, as Graham and Sánchez note:

> In spite of its own long and painful history of underdevelopment, economic emigration, and otherness, far from recognizing a commonality and attempting to integrate the experience of the marginalized into it self-proclaimedly pluralistic culture, [Spain] has instead assumed the stance of "First World" Europe. It is almost as if constructing and adopting the same "others" or outgroups as the rest were considered the hallmark of Spain's membership of the "club" . . . But in opting for assimilation on these terms, Spanish policy is contributing to the build-up of a social and political climate which encourages racism and xenophobia. For in Spain, as elsewhere, it is precisely that migrant minority which is paying most heavily, with health, and increasingly its lives, for the modernization process.[18]

El Cadáver's warning therefore reflects Spain's anxieties about maintaining its relatively new status as a European power. Upon joining the European Union, Spain was finally able to combat the often cited expression *África empieza en los Pirineos* (Africa begins in the Pyrenees). As Antumi Toasije succinctly notes, despite the long-standing contributions of Africans to Spanish culture, "With the Europeanization process in Spain, the contribution of Africans, the fact of the Africanity of Spain, and the importance of Black communities and elements to Spanish history have been definitively wiped out from the official discourse."[19] This erasure from national discourse eliminates the possibility for cross-cultural empathy and contributes to the overall autochthonous fear of the Other embodied in the image of the black man.

El Cadáver's warning from the afterlife is symbolic of Spain's rejection of Africa in order to further its own (trans)national interests, grounded in Spain's simultaneous fear of the Other and fear of being othered. This phobogenic reality, as El Cadáver explains, will ultimately lead to Ombasi's death:

> Te ahogarás en la miseria y en las enfermedades, en el pis y en el hollín . . . Dormirás bajo tierra sin estar muerto, oliendo a orines y

> todos pasarán esquivando tu mirada. Algunos se reirán de ti, otros te despreciarán, otros te humillarán, otros te pegarán, otros te tendrán miedo y los que se creen mejor te tendrán lástima. (*LMHO*, 66)
>
> You'll drown in misery and illness, in dirt and piss . . . You'll sleep underground, still alive, smelling like urine, and every passerby will turn away from you. Some will laugh at you, some will despise you, some will hit you, others will be afraid of you, and those that think they're better than you will pity you. (*DMG*, 24)

Ombasi disregards this foreshadowing of his fate in the metro of Madrid as pessimistic banter fabricated by those who have failed in order to discourage migrants who are still in pursuit of their dreams. Despite Ombasi's disregard for the warning, the importance of this excerpt is the Spanish treatment of the migrant. The imagery created here situates the black migrant at a subterranean and subhuman level, akin to that of a subway rat. In so doing, he is a personification of vermin that must be eradicated from the metro so that passengers may commute without perturbation.

Out of fear that Ombasi will hurt them, upon waking up, the family heads back to their car. At the same time, the drizzle has converted into a storm. Ombasi wishes to go with them, but his inability to communicate obscures this objective. Antonio finds his spark plug in the lining of his jacket and rushes back to meet the rest of his family at the car, telling Ombasi, "Y más vale que te vuelvas a la selva, que aquí pegas menos que un pulpo en un garaje" (You better go back to the jungle because here you're just a fish out of water) (*LMHO*, 78; *DMG*, 29). This statement uncovers the father's racism, as well as his views on multicultural integration. The assumption that Ombasi comes from the jungle is a long-standing stereotype of Africans meant to equate them with animals or savage peoples. These stereotypes are promoted in Spanish popular culture through products such as Conguitos and Cola-Cao, whose respective iconographies project the image of Africans as savages in the jungles or deserts. The second clause of his declaration insinuates that as an African, Ombasi cannot exist within the Spanish context. This rhetorical exclusion shows a progression of racism, from one based on skin color to one based on cultural compatibility, thereby culminating in Antonio's desire to keep Ombasi away from his family and from Spain.

Masculine tension explodes in scene 13 when the family tries to drive away and Ombasi jumps onto the hood of the car, prompting Antonio to exit the car to fight him. This fight, however, ends up doing more damage to El Padre than to Ombasi. The stage directions note:

> *El Padre sigue golpeando a Ombasi, el cual responde a los golpes. Ruedan por la arena. La Madre trata de ayudar a su marido. Baja del coche y coge la barra, tratando de golpear a barullo, terminado por darle en la espalda a su marido, que grita de dolor. El Niño baja*

también del coche y empieza a arrojar arena a OMBASI *con regulares resultados, pues parte va a caer en los ojos del padre.* (LMHO, 93)

FATHER continues to beat OMBASI, who in turn responds to his blows. THEY roll in the sand. MOTHER tries to help her husband. SHE gets out of the car, picks up the bar, tries to strike hard, but ends up hitting her husband on the back. FATHER shrieks in pain. The BOY also gets out of the car and starts throwing sand at OMBASI with mediocre results, as some of it falls in FATHER's eyes. (DMG, 37)

The violence intended for Ombasi actually ends up hurting El Padre, such that their violence symbolizes the national inner turmoil in Spain that has erupted as a result of immigration shifting the nation's cultural and racial demographics. This inner conflict is later confirmed when El Cadáver tells Ombasi in the afterlife that El Padre's impetus for fighting Ombasi was hatred because "Se odiaba a sí mismo" (He hated himself) (*LMHO*, 97; *DMG*, 39). This self-hate is a result of El Padre's inability to uphold standards of masculinity that his roles of husband, father, and breadwinner required. His deep-rooted frustration thus manifests itself through violence. As a result, there is great irony when La Madre and El Niño inflict damage on El Padre, as he verbally and physically abuses them throughout the play. This inversion of *machista* violence is the final blow against his masculinity, ultimately leaving him with nothing, since, as revealed in the final scene, he loses sight in one eye and his family has abandoned him.

The arrival of the Civil Guard helicopter at the end of scene 13 is a clear example of the Spanish state exerting its sovereignty and necropolitical power. The arrest of Ombasi is not shown on stage, but we learn in the final scene that Ombasi is deported and makes the journey again. On the second trip, Ombasi makes it to Madrid but gets sick from the cold weather there:

OMBASI. Estaba tosiendo, y me dolía la cabeza. Tenía calor. Hacía frío, pero yo tenía calor. Me mareé. Me caí.

EL CADÁVER. En un charco. Te quedaste caído en el charco y te ahogaste. Lo que yo te dije.[20] (*LMHO*, 96)

OMBASI. I was coughing, and my head hurt. I was hot. It was cold, but I was hot. I got dizzy. I fell down.

BODY. In a puddle. You'd fallen down in a puddle and drowned. Just like I told you. People walked by and watched. And you drowned.[21]

Scene 14's title and location, "Una playa. A orillas del mar de la nada" (A Beach along a Shore of Nothingness), indicate a purgatorial space that is neither Europe nor Africa, which allows the play to come full circle in that the presence of the dead on the beach begins and ends the play. The beach is, therefore, the border, or liminal space, between life and death, through which migrants such as Ombasi hope to traverse.[22] Unfortunately for Ombasi, Spain's necropolitics impede his survival, but it is presented as very much his own fault: "Pero ya que te deportaron, deberías haberte quedado. No todos tienen una segunda oportunidad" (Since you were deported, you should've stayed. Not everyone gets a second chance) (*LMHO*, 96; *DMG*, 38). Ombasi's second chance in Africa, alive, was not enough; this is a reflection of the journeys of many migrants who are deported simply to try again, only to be left to die along the way or within Spain.

While the text does not necessarily lend itself as such, many have interpreted the mise-en-scène as a comedy. According to the playwright, audiences in Madrid laughed hysterically at the depiction of the Spanish family as uncouth and ignorant, which he attributes to the average theatergoer in Madrid being of high socioeconomic means and primarily leftist. When the play was staged in the Madrid suburb of Móstoles, however, there was a notable decrease in laughter as its audience was much more working class, thus perhaps identified more with the family on stage. In a personal interview with del Moral, he states that unintentionally creating a comedy at the expense of working-class people is one of his regrets about the play. Another shift from the text to performance that ultimately affected its interpretation by audiences was the use of adult actors to play the two children's roles. The result was an exaggerated representation of youth that distracted from the fear the two children had of their parents and of Ombasi, thereby exacerbating the caricature of the Spanish family, which shifts the play's focus from the tensions surrounding immigration to the shocking family dysfunction. Ombasi is left as the only well-rounded character, whose portrayal evokes the shock of the *patera* phenomenon as it was beginning in the early 1990s.

La mirada del hombre oscuro is the first theatrical foray into African migration and the cadavers that would begin to line the floors of the Atlantic and Mediterranean, as well as the shores of Spain (and other Southern European nations). This motif expands and metamorphoses in the other plays that will be discussed in this chapter. Death is portrayed as Ombasi's destiny, despite his well-intentioned logic for wanting to reach Spain. His death is facilitated by the ignorance, racism, and overall lack of empathy personified in the Spanish family and the metro passengers who leave him to die alone. If death is proposed as the solution to the impending migratory phenomenon, then the state and society are complicit in these deaths that only became more common in years subsequent to the debut of this play.

Whose Death Is It Anyway? Metatheater and Complicity in *La falsa muerte de Jaro el Negro*

The complicity of Spanish society in the daily occurrence of African migrants' deaths is explored through a roller coaster of emotional positioning in Fernando Martín Iniesta's 1997 metatheatrical play *La falsa muerte de Jaro el*

Negro. Although the play delves into the xenophobia and racism of 1990s Spain through the presence of skinheads that kill the title character, what makes this play truly necropolitical is the incorporation of the audience as unknowing actors at the play's beginning and end. Through the use of metatheater, spectators become active bystanders, if not participants, in the social exclusion and subsequent murder of Jaro.[23] This participation therefore forces the audience to question its complicity in antiblackness and the violence it engenders. The blurred line between the play and real life is intended to demonstrate that migrant death cannot simply serve as entertainment for the Spanish populace when those same deaths are glossed over in real life.

The play is divided into four scenes including a prologue and an epilogue. In the prologue, Jaro strolls through the aisles of the theater trying to sell merchandise to audience members until the Acomodador (Usher) scolds him and yells at him to leave before the show begins. In scene 1, three skinheads, Himmert, Weber, and La Pija (The Posh Girl) discuss their reasons for becoming skinheads and their objective to make Spain a better, whiter nation. Their leader, El Duce, arrives to give them a mission to go out and rid the streets of the "scum" that impedes on the lives of good (white) people. In scene 2, the group of skinheads encounters Jaro after a prosperous day of sales, surrounding him so he cannot escape, and brutally attack him. As the stage directions note, *"Empiezan a golpearle salvajemente, se oyen sus gritos de terror, brillan las navajas y crujen las cadenas"* (*They start to savagely beat him, his screams of terror can be heard, blades flash and chains clank*).[24] In the epilogue, Autor (Author) appears to tell the audience that the show is over and then directs the actors to return to their dressing rooms. All the actors leave except the one who plays Jaro, who remains stretched out on the ground. This act of disobedience causes Autor to rebuke him, "Levántate que vea el respetable que tu muerte ha sido la falsa muerte de Jaro el Negro" (Stand up so that the respectable audience can see that your death was merely the false death of Jaro the Negro) (*LFMJN*, 133). After some resistance, the actor leaves and Autor has a final word with the audience, directing them to applaud, if they wish.

Despite its brevity, *La falsa muerte de Jaro el Negro* is packed with sociopolitical and necropolitical messages. The play begins with the exclusion of Jaro from the cultural space (the theater), implying a hegemonic view of what culture is and to whom it belongs. Jaro, having purchased a ticket to the performance, mistakenly believes this allows him to sell his merchandise in the theater, stating "Y Jaro pagar para poder vender . . . Todo legal . . . Todo con papeles" (And Jaro pay in order to be able to sell . . . All legal . . . All with papers) (*LFMJN*, 120). The legality of his presence, both in the theater and in Spain (as he has a ticket and documentation), are nullified by his vending. The Acomodador's reproach, "Aquí está prohibido vender. Esto es un teatro" (Selling is prohibited here. This is a theater), ironically articulates a disregard for the purpose of a theater, to market an artistic vision via theatrical performance (*LFMJN*, 120). As Jaro is not understood to be part of the performance, he and his merchandise are ejected from the theater, because his presence is a disruption to the "actual" pending performance, as noted by the usher's final line, "¡Salga de una vez! . . . Va a empezar la representación" (Leave at once! . . . The show is about to begin) (*LFMJN*, 120). This scene constitutes the first stage of the play's emotional position in that the spectators' reaction to Jaro's vending and subsequent removal from the theater likely aligns with their view of his presence as a nuisance. Therefore, what is allowed to be sold to the spectator is not Jaro's tangible merchandise but rather antiblackness and racial violence. Through this metatheatrical scene, Jaro is simultaneously an explicit vendor and an implicit cultural commodity to be consumed by a cautionary Spanish audience.

Jaro's exile from the theater aisles facilitates the spectators' consumption of the play's focus on neo-Nazi violence. This focus is immediately made apparent from the set design, which according to the stage directions we can see *"en las paredes, pósters que reflejan violencia, enseñas nazis, Doctor Martee's [*sic*], bomber, etc."* (*on the walls, posters that show violence, Nazi symbols, Doc Martens, bomber jackets, etc.*) (*LFMJN*, 121). Even before the three protagonists say their first lines, we are made aware of their allegiance to neo-Nazi ideology because as Esteban Ibarra outlines in his book *Los crímenes del odio: Violencia skin y neonazi en España*, "Se les reconoce generalmente por sus cabezas rapadas o por llevar el pelo muy corto, sus tatuajes, simbología y eslóganes nazis, y un «uniforme» compuesto por botas de combate, vaqueros cortos, tirantes y cazadoras Bomber" (Neo-Nazis can generally be recognized for their shaved heads or very short hair, their tattoos, Nazi symbology and slogans, and a "uniform" composed of combat boots, jean shorts, suspenders, and bomber jackets).[25] As Ibarra explains, neo-Nazism emerged in Spain in the mid-1980s:

> Entre los factores objetivos que facilitan el resurgimiento del racismo, la xenofobia, el antisemitismo y otras manifestaciones relacionadas de intolerancia en Europa, hay que señalar las transformaciones y contradicciones que están produciéndose en el viejo continente: la crisis económica internacional, la presión migratoria y los movimientos demográficos, el temor y la inseguridad por el futuro ante el desempleo y la pobreza. (*LFMJN*, 24)

> Among the factors that facilitate the resurgence of the racism, xenophobia, anti-Semitism, and other related manifestations of intolerance in Europe, it is important to note the transformations and contradictions that are occurring on the old continent: the international economic crisis, migratory pressure, and demographic movements, fear and insecurity about the future in the face of unemployment and poverty.

All of these factors formed a backdrop for the scapegoating that skinheads use to justify their discrimination and violence. Unlike the use of humor to portray prejudice in *La mirada del hombre ocsuro*, this play aims to depict the serious depravity of those who follow neo-Nazi ideology.

As seen in other plays concerning neo-Nazi youth (such as *Cachorros de negro mirar* by Paloma Pedrero and *Mane, Thecel, Phares* by Borja Ortiz de Gondra), the male protagonists are not known in the text by their real names and take great offense at their enunciation. We see this when Himmert mistakenly calls Weber "Pablo," "¡Coño con el Pablo! . . . ¿Se te ha vuelto a olvidar que me llamo Weber? . . . We-ber . . . Y tú, Himmert, que nos hemos cambiado los nombres para que no nos identifiquen si nos trincan" (Fucking stop with Pablo! . . . Have you forgotten again that my name is Weber? We-ber . . . And you're Himmert. We changed our names so that they can't identify us if we get arrested) (*LFMJN*, 121). While this appears to be a good plan, if they were actually arrested, Spanish law enforcement would surely be able to identify their legal names on their DNI (documento nacional de identidad), by taking fingerprints, or both.

Interestingly enough, La Pija does not have a German name but rather a Spanish nickname that reveals her high socioeconomic class. Offended by her lack of a German name, she complains about another squad member with a Spanish name, "Eugenio." Unbeknownst to her, however, "Eugenio" is also an admired name within neo-Nazi groups because as Weber explains:

> Lo cuenta en un libro un tío que no sé cómo se llama . . . Un día, dos de mayo, se entrena de que, para celebrar el día que los franceses fusilaron a los españoles, las autoridades han organizado una fiesta en la que se bailan pasodobles y se tiran fuegos artificiales. El tío se cabrea «Cuando la Patria está agonizando, puteada por sus hijos y medio muerta, estos cabrones quieren enterrarla con pasodobles.» Como ahora está pasando, que la Patria la pisan los comunistas . . . [. . .] Pues Eugenio cogió una pistola y se cargó a no sé quién mientras gritaba que así se proclamaba la primavera de España. (*LFMJN*, 122)

> Some guy whose name I don't know tells the story in a book . . . One day, May 2nd, he finds out that to celebrate the day that the French executed the Spanish, the local authorities had organized a party to dance *pasodobles* and launch fireworks. The guy gets pissed off and says, "When the Nation is agonizing, screwed by its children and half dead, these assholes want to bury her with *pasodobles*." Like what's happening now, with the Nation overrun by communists . . . [. . .] Well, Eugenio grabbed a pistol and shot someone while shouting that this is how to proclaim the spring of Spain.

The book to which Weber refers is Rafael García Serrano's 1938 novel *Eugenio o Proclamación de la Primavera*, in which this scene takes place.[26]

García Serrano dedicated this text to José Antonio Primo de Rivera, founder of the Falange Española (Spanish Phalanx party), and had hoped to deliver it to him personally, but Primo de Rivera was killed before the novel was completed. As Eugenio G. de Nora explains, the novel is considered to be one of the great profascist works written during the Spanish Civil War because it is "un verdadero manifiesto . . . de los ideales de la Falange" (a true manifesto . . . of the ideals of the Falange).[27] The interpolation of the novel into the neo-Nazi plot of the play provides the teens with ideological role models from Spanish history, now embodied in their group leaders. In addition, some spectators may pick up on the literary reference and its role in the Franco regime's literary canon.

As they continue to take turns smoking a joint, the group begins to discuss their ideology and their commitment to it. Weber declares:

> Somos la estatua del Comendador, la última esperanza de la Patria, la reserva espiritual de Occidente, los que creemos en las profundas diferencias entre los hombres y los grupos de hombres y luchamos por la preferencia nacional, y, si nos declaran la guerra los que dicen que todos los hombres son iguales, tendrán guerra. (*LFMJN*, 123)
>
> We are the statue of the Comendador, the last hope for the homeland, the spiritual reserve of the West, those who believe in the profound differences between men and groups of men, and we fight for national preference. And if those who say that all men are equal declare war on us, they will face war.

The ideology Weber articulates depends on ethnocentrism and difference to sustain itself. The former is the basis of eugenic thought, through which the group can claim superiority over other groups. The latter provides the target for extermination to create the utopian white society they desire. Within Spain's current political structure, such groups are considered fringe extremists because as Weber states: "¡La democracia es una mierda! ¿Sabes qué dice la democracia? Pues que todos somos iguales. ¡No te jode! ¿Soy yo igual que el maricón ese al que atizamos la otra noche?" (Democracy is bullshit! Do you know what democracy states? That we are all equal. No fucking way! I'm equal to that fag we beat up the other night?) (*LFMJN*, 123). For their ideology to thrive, there would need to be an infiltration of the political structure that would establish national credibility for their existence. In the play, however, the skinheads function more as organized crime groups than as a political movement.

The play makes clear the connection between 1990s neo-Nazism and the dying fascism of the 1970s and 1980s. For example, when Weber explains his father's hopes for Spain and Weber's future:

> Mi padre era coronel y estaba a punto de ascender a general, cuando llegó la democracia. . . . Desde entonces, no ha salido a la calle y

> dice que el aire de España está infectado por las banderas rojas, las hoces, los martillos y el aliento de los comunistas y es irrespirable para un hombre de honor. . . . No vayas a la Academia. El sitio para luchar por España está hoy en la calle, en la clandestinidad. Los verdaderos patriotas tiene que esconderse. La lucha debe seguir sin uniforme. Estamos rodeados de traidores, traidores que, muerto el Caudillo, dieron la espalda a su obra, traidores que dejaron solo a Tejero, ese día glorioso del 23F. . . . Vuestra misión es resucitarla con la sangre si es preciso, con la muerte, si es necesario. Os ha tocado en suerte ser los defensores de una sagrada intolerancia y de una hermosa intransigencia. Que sean vuestras armas . . . Si las calles están sucias, limpiadlas. Que algún día vuestros hijos puedan respirar en una España major. (*LFMJN*, 126–27)

> My father was a colonel and was about to be promoted to general when democracy arrived. . . . Since then, he hasn't left the house and says that Spain's air is infected by red flags, sickles, hammers, and the breath of communists, which is unbreathable for a man of honor. . . . Don't go to the Academy. The place to fight for Spain today is in the streets, in secrecy. The true patriots have to hide. The flight continues without uniforms. We are surrounded by traitors. Traitors who, now that el Caudillo is dead, turned their backs on his work, traitors who left Tejero alone, that glorious day, February 23rd. . . . Your mission is to resuscitate it with blood, if need be, with death, if necessary. You have the luck of being the defenders of a sacred intolerance and a beautiful intransigence. Those are your weapons . . . If the streets are dirty, clean them, so one day your children can breathe in a better Spain.

This excerpt demonstrates that the link between Francoism and neo-Nazism is not far-fetched, as both are exclusionist, nationalist movements rooted in racism as a core of their ideologies. In his chapter "Racism and Nationalism" in *Race, Nation, Class: Ambiguous Identities* (1991), Etienne Balibar makes clear that nationalism cannot be removed from racism because sovereignty depends so much on defining who is *not* part of the nation.[28] In a similar fashion, necropolitics implies that sovereignty depends on the death of the unwanted Other and the survival of those who are desired citizens.

The play's inner plot (scenes 1 and 2) demonstrates that Spain has not escaped the depths of the Franco regime's fascist ideology, which has mutated in a way that is "clandestine" and more explicitly racist. Weber's father is simply transferring his dream of total homogeneity, which the Falange Española referred to as *unidad de destino*, to his son.[29] To anchor the transition from Francoism to neo-Nazism, Weber says that his father, "habló de mí a alguien de «Galaxia» y me dijo dónde tenía que presentarme . . . Y por eso, estoy en el comando" (spoke about me to someone from "Galaxia" and told me where I had to introduce myself . . . And that's why I'm in the squad) (*LFMJN*, 127). Galaxia refers to Operación Galaxia, the code name for the plan to stage a coup against the Spanish democratic government during the Transition, which took place on February 23, 1981. Due to this failed coup, those allegiant to Franco and his fascist ideology had to revert to underground admiration and implementation of those ideals. It is for this reason that Weber's father would know exactly to whom to send his son for membership in a neo-Nazi squadron.

As Francoist fascism serves as a springboard for the Spanish neo-Nazi movements of the 1990s, it should come as no surprise that the three adolescents are led by a man known as "El Duce," whose code name is a Hispanicized version of the title that Benito Mussolini gave himself as the leader of Fascist Italy (1922–1945). As a leader of this neo-Nazi squad, El Duce functions as an ideological and professional mentor for the trio. He also serves as the middleman between them and his superior, El Camarada (The Comrade), who never appears on stage. The name is a reference to José Antonio Primo de Rivera, founder of the Falange Española. As an embodiment of the Spanish fascist leader, it makes sense that he is the one who gives the teens their mission for the night: "Aúna a ese grupo de valientes y sal con ellos a limpiar la mierda que infecta las calles para que puedan respirar los hombres de bien" (Gather up that group of valiant soldiers and go out with them to clean out the shit that infects the streets, so that good men can breathe) (*LFMJN*, 129). As Ibarra notes: "Los mayores mandan pero no ejecutan, y son los más jóvenes los que van armados con navajas, puños americanos y otros enseres para dar los golpes. De esta manera, los más veteranos skins . . . salvan su responsabilidad y logran que la violencia siga en la calle" (The older members give commands but do not execute them. It is rather the young members who go armed with knives, brass knuckles, and other tools to deliver beatings. In this way, the most veteran skinheads . . . escape responsibility and ensure that violence continues in the streets).[30] This delegation of action also gives younger members a sense of ownership in the goals and mission of their cause, thus creating the ideological fervor necessary to brutalize and even kill victims.

The murder of Jaro in scene 2 marks the acceleration from racist rhetoric to brazen violence. El Duce begins by asking Jaro, "¿Has visto por aquí a un mono asqueroso?" (Have you seen a disgusting monkey around here?) (*LFMJN*, 130). At first, Jaro does not understand that "monkey" refers to him, but once he does, he attempts to get away from the group, stating that he is on his way home. The group prevents his escape and the squadron leader tells him that his presence is prohibited:

JARO. ¿Todo prohibido para Jaro?

EL DUCE. Prohibido que vayas por este sitio, prohibido por ese otro, prohibido que te quedes aquí. ¿Lo has entendido?

JARO. No.
EL DUCE. Que esta calle, esta ciudad, este país está prohibido para los que huelen a mono, como tú.
JARO. Jaro legal, Jaro tener papeles. (*Los saca.*)
. . .
EL DUCE. Pues oye, Jaro, esos papeles y los que te los han dado son basura de la misma clase. (*LFMJN*, 131)

JARO. Everything forbidden for Jaro?
EL DUCE. Forbidden that you go this way, forbidden that way, forbidden that you stay here. Got it?
JARO. No.
EL DUCE. This street, this city, this country is forbidden to those that smell like monkey, like you.
JARO. Jaro legal, Jaro have papers. (*He takes them out.*)
. . .
EL DUCE. Listen, Jaro, those papers and those who gave them to you are the same type of trash.

As in the prologue, Jaro's legality does not permit his presence; in fact, it does not even grant him a right to live. Jaro's blackness not only indicts him but also all those who made his presence in Spain possible (e.g., immigration officers and the liberal government laws). Analogous to Ombasi's subhuman death as a subway "rat" in the Madrid metro, Jaro's death is preceded by stripping his humanity, calling him a "monkey."

This erasure or discrediting of Jaro's humanity is a rhetorical example of what Christina Sharpe calls "living in the wake":

> Put another way, living in the wake means living in and with terror in that in much of what passes for public discourse *about* terror we, Black people, become the *carriers* of terror, terror's embodiment, and not the primary object of terror's multiple enactments; the ground of terror's possibility globally. This is everywhere clear as we think about . . . those Black people transmigrating the African continent towards the Mediterranean and then to Europe who are imagined as insects, swarms, vectors of disease.[31]

Sharpe's positioning of antiblackness as a global phenomenon highlights racist discourse's sinister ability to place blame on the victim, such that black people embody rather than endure terror, thereby making them responsible for their own tragedies. This tactic, used in the context of immigration to Europe, unfortunately continues to dehumanize black people, rendering them unworthy of sympathy.

Jaro's death presents the second stage of emotional positioning: pity and disassociation. The spectator, upon witnessing the horrific verbal and physical attack on Jaro, is moved to pity him as a victim of a senseless act. However, as neo-Nazi groups in Spain at the time were widely seen as fringe extremists and unruly teens, there is also the capacity for the spectator to completely disregard the scene's violence as an exaggeration of reality. It is therefore possible that the Spanish spectator defensively disassociates from those characters in an effort to maintain a progressive facade, in which case sympathy for Jaro functions merely as a way to disconnect from the skinhead characters.

Sympathy is abruptly cut short as the epilogue begins with Autor running out on stage to announce the play's "end": "¡La función ha terminado! . . . Aplaudan ustedes si creen que esto . . . esto . . . , lo que ha acontecido en el escenario, merece un aplauso (*Pausa que da lugar a la reflexión. Dirigiéndose a los actores*)" (The show has ended! . . . Applaud if you believe that this . . . this . . . , what took place on stage, deserves an applause. [*Pause that leads to reflection. Turning toward the actors*]) (*LFMJN*, 133).The reflective pause not only allows spectators to collect themselves after a horrific scene but also to reflect on their relationship to the characters, Jaro in particular. The pause may be a eureka moment for some, who finally realize that the man who was selling merchandise in the aisles is the same man who was just killed by the skinheads. This realization symbolizes the third stage of emotional positioning: a reconciliation of one's attitude toward Jaro the vendor versus Jaro the victim. This juxtaposition presents a paradox if one applauds Jaro's ejection and mourns his death minutes later.

This spectatorial paradox is a clear example of what theater scholar Bernard Beckerman calls "empathetic parallelism." As he explains: "Imaginatively we follow a path that runs parallel, not to the events themselves, but to the shifts of tension either between characters or between ourselves and the performers. This process may be called *empathetic parallelism*: where the audience is engaged fully in a presentation, that is, where the interaction is sustained from beginning to end, the responsive path parallels the entire work."[32] *La falsa muerte de Jaro el Negro* relies on spectators' interaction and engagement with the plot to reach an empathetic end based in self-reflection. As the tension between the audience and Jaro continuously shifts throughout the play, one's sense of empathy must shift in parallel. These shifts may be more or less severe depending on the group affect among the spectators during a particular performance.

The paradox is further complicated when Autor then tells the actors to exit and strip all semblance of their characters, "Hagan mutis y diríjanse a los vestuarios y en el espejo que hay en los camerinos, al verse la cara, antes de comentar con sus compañeros cómo ha sido la representación, quítense, con todo cuidado, el maquillaje, que no les quede ni una leve sombra, para evitar que se les identifique con los personajes que han representado" (Exit and head to the dressing rooms, and in the mirror that's in there, as soon as you see your face, before speaking to your colleagues about how the show went, remove your makeup very carefully, removing the last, faintest trace, so that you are not identified as the characters you represented) (*LFMJN*, 133). Breaking character allows the actors to be able to decompress from the gravity of their roles. Breaking character is not so easy for the black actor, however, as he cannot strip his race as easily as the white actors can strip their ideological mask. Recognition that the actor who plays Jaro continues to be a black man outside of the theatrical space marks the fourth stage of the play's emotional positioning. To leave the stage is to possibly expose himself to the violence of antiblackness in the real world, and perhaps for that reason he refuses to leave.

As the actor remains on the floor, in essence he is a martyr. He dies as "Jaro" to persuade the spectator of the value of black life, as Jaro's horrific death provokes sympathy. Autor's wish for him to leave the stage and to strip off the identity of Jaro, however, is an effort to downplay and trivialize racist violence, and thus the actor's initial refusal can be read as a metatheatrical act of resistance. Autor proclaims that Jaro's death is fake, "Sólo teatro, magia, juego, mentira . . . ¡Teatro al fin y al cabo! . . . Sólo eso: teatro. Anda . . . (*Repite el nombre del actor.*) Date unas vuelta, que vean que estás vivo" (Only theater, magic, games, lies . . . Theater in the end! Just that: theater. Come on . . . [*Repeats the actor's name.*] Do a few turns so they see you're alive) (*LFMJN*, 133–34). Since this is a theatrical work, we know Jaro is not real and his death is an artistic creation, but if theater is supposed to represent the world we live in, then Autor is, in fact, upending the purpose of theater by rupturing the fourth wall through which we observe. He attempts to establish inurement in the spectator, similar to the desensitization that occurs with recurring images of African migrants' deaths in Spanish mass media. Susan Sontag notes: "People don't become inured to what they are shown . . . because of the *quantity* of images dumped on them. It is passivity that dulls feeling."[33] The spectator's inability to help Jaro, becoming a bystander to his death, provokes both horror and pity, but ultimately it lends itself to passivity. Therefore, the actor's resistance serves to insist on theater's sociological importance as an artistic microcosm of the world.

The black actor's classical training provides him with rhetorical arguments to debate Autor's attempt to dismiss him. As a last resort, the black actor wishes to have a word with the audience but is reproached again by Autor:

> "No. Eso tan bonito del tinglado de la vieja farsa no es de esta función . . ." (*El Negro vuelve a insistirle al oído.*) "¡El gran teatro del mundo! . . . ¡Basta ya de tópicos de lugares comunes y de pereza mental . . . ! El mundo no es un teatro . . . aunque el teatro sí es un mundo . . . o debiera serlo." (*Hace un gesto imperativo y el Negro se marcha.*) (*LFMJN*, 134)

> No. That really pretty (monologue) about the mummer of the old farce is not meant for this performance . . . *(The* B*LACK* M*AN again insists, whispers in his ear.)* The great theater of the world! . . . Enough with clichés of common places and of mental laziness . . . ! The world is not a theater . . . even though the theater is indeed a world . . . or it should be. (*He makes an imperative gesture and the* B*LACK* M*AN leaves.*)

The black actor whispers references to two canonical plays: Jacinto Benavente's *Los intereses creados* (1907) and Pedro Calderón de la Barca's *El gran teatro del mundo* (1655).[34] Both plays are social critiques that imply, through secular and religious vantage points, respectively, that the world is but a stage on which we are all actors. The desire to recite from these plays reflects the actor's insistence that theater functions as a didactical tool through which social injustices, such as racism, can be fought. Autor, on the other hand, believes that theater's main purpose is to distract from those injustices through entertainment.

Upon the black actor's surrender and retreat, Autor speaks the last lines of the play, "Ya pueden ustedes aplaudir, si lo desean . . . El teatro, para vivir, necesita del éxito . . . para no morir . . . de la realidad, y ésta, a veces, no se merece un aplauso" (You can applaud now, if you wish . . . In order to live, theater needs success . . . to not die . . . from reality, and this sometimes does not deserve applause) (*LFMJN*, 135). Following Autor's logic, the world cannot be a theater, because if it were, it would require applauding reality, which does not always deserve praise. This final declaration cements the final emotional position, in which the audience is left to contemplate its role in applauding xenophobia, antiblackness, and violence.

La falsa muerte de Jaro el Negro employs a necropolitical narrative structure that systematically critiques the spectator as a participant in antiblackness. Death in this play serves as a point from which a critique of Spanish society can be articulated. The use of metatheater facilitates an emotional journey that ends with reflection rather than inurement. By doing so, the play's message regarding antiblackness and black migrants' deaths in Spain is clear: passivity is complicity.

Death, Soccer, and the Innocence of the Global South in *Friday*

In recent years, there has been an alarming increase in deaths of Africans making the journey to Spain by sea. In response to the Spanish public's tendency toward inurement to these deaths, to provoke compassion artists have taken new approaches to conceptualize death.[35] Irma Correa's 2011 play, *Friday*, forms part of that artistic resistance by exploring this migratory trend from a different lens, that of a child.[36] Although she is not the first to do this, her work is the only full-length play to use African children as the migrant protagonists.[37] The play is based on a true story of a Nigerian teenager named Friday who traversed the Atlantic with five of his friends with the hope of reaching Spain to one day play for FC Barcelona like his hero, Lionel Messi. This story was documented in *El País* on November 17, 2007, in an article entitled, "El niño polizón que sueña con Messi" (The Child Stowaway Who Dreams about Messi). The news article begins by painting a negative image of Friday and his humanity, stating, "No sabe leer ni escribir. Aparenta estar aún muy impactado por lo que ha vivido y no entiende nada de lo que ocurre a su alrededor. Friday T. asegura que el 15 de diciembre cumplirá 15 años. La prueba ósea de su muñeca certifica que apenas tiene 13" (He doesn't know how to read or write. He appears to still be quite affected by what he has lived through and does not understand anything around him. Friday T. insists that he will turn fifteen on December 15. The bone tests of his wrist certify that he is barely thirteen years old).[38] Friday's purported criminality described at the beginning of the article effectively negates the sense of empathy that the rest of the article attempts to engender. It is for this very reason that plays like *Friday* are so important: to humanize the stories of migrant children who have been dehumanized by society.

The play is composed of twenty scenes that alternate between Friday's time in Nigeria leading up to his stowing away and his experiences with Gabriel and Emeka on the oil tanker en route to the Canary Islands. Both narrative tracks are woven together by Friday's dream of playing for FC Barcelona. Friday is from a poor Yoruba fishing village in southern Nigeria that recently has been polluted by the booming oil industry. He lives with his brother Olusegun, his mother, and his aunt and uncle. Friday is obsessed with soccer, skipping school to practice with a ball made from rags, as he cannot afford to buy a standard ball. He is also extremely protective of his mother, who is dying from a sexually transmitted disease, likely HIV/AIDS, given that Olusegun says, "Enfermedad triste y asquerosa, que chupa la sangre hasta dejar los cuerpos secos. Ellos dicen que todo se puede acabar si usamos el plástico. Antes de unirse hombre y mujer, el plástico" (A sad and disgusting disease that sucks blood until it leaves the body dry. They say that it could all end if we use the plastic. Before men and women join together, [use] the plastic).[39] Upon her death, Tío (Uncle) decides to sell the boys to a cacao farm up north to build a new well in the village. While en route to the north, Olusegun and Friday escape from the truck and make their way south to a port city, which we can assume to be Lagos. Once there, they find themselves in a pickpocketing ring led by Funto and his minions, Maliki and Gani. The brothers escape Funto's lair with Gani to meet with Ojkwu, who claims to have a good price on trips to Europe. Ojkwu, however, is simply a bounty hunter for Oso, an older smuggler, who has a lust for young boys. Oso sexually assaults Friday, but when he attempts to do the same to Olusegun, a chaotic fight breaks out in which everyone dies except Friday. From this moment until Friday's presence on the oil tanker, we have no textual information to understand how he arrived.

The second narrative stream follows Friday's sea journey in which he is hidden in the axel of the oil tanker's helm alongside Emeka and Gabriel. Given the age difference between the three (Emeka and Gabriel are in their twenties and thirties, respectively), Friday's innocence is more striking juxtaposed against the other two men. The three have several conversations about Spain and what life will be like once they arrive. In addition, we witness Friday suffer through seasickness, hunger, and dehydration, all the while continuing to hold on to his beloved cloth soccer ball. The play tragically ends with the drowning of Friday, just as the light of the La Entellada lighthouse (Canary Islands) comes into view. This play demonstrates the stark reality that children who attempt to make the journey to Europe are the most susceptible to abuse and death along the way. For the purpose of this chapter, however, I shall examine the role that soccer plays in creating value and false hope for children like Friday, leading them to risk their lives for a dream that will likely never come true.

The play begins with Friday entering the stage while playing with a soccer ball made from rags, symbolizing the extreme poverty of his hometown in Nigeria, but later also symbolizing his sense of security and hope along the journey. His lack of a real soccer ball, in his mind, is holding him back from becoming the player he sees within himself. The stage directions, however, state: "*Entra Friday, con una leve cojera. Coge la pelota. Juega. Mal*" (*Friday enters, with a slight limp. He grabs the ball. He plays. Badly*) (Correa, *Friday*, 13). In spite of his limp, he truly believes in himself as a soccer player of great acclaim. Friday's disability and his awareness (or lack thereof) of it shape his dream and his journey. He even skips school to spend more time practicing his skills, even though his mother tells him, "Tu cuerpo no está hecho para juegos" (Your body is not made for games) (23). His determination to achieve fame in the West through soccer is by no means a new phenomenon as African players have played for top European teams for years.

What makes Friday's case distinct is that his disability in fact perpetuates the notion that he is an amazing soccer player. In scene 4, he declares, "Soy el mejor futbolista del mundo. Dicen que soy cojo. Que tengo una pierna más corta que la otra. Yo no lo noto. O sí, a veces. Pero camino y corro como los demás. En realidad, no. En realidad soy más rápido" (I am the best soccer player in the world. They say that I'm crippled. That I have one leg that's shorter than the other. I don't notice it. Oh, well sometimes, yes. But I walk and run just like everyone else. In reality, no. In reality, I'm faster) (23). His naïveté, perhaps to be expected in a child his age, is also fueled by the story of his hero, Lionel Messi. As a child, the famed Argentine soccer player suffered from growth hormone deficiency that stunted his growth. He began hormone treatment in Argentina, but when the costs soared, FC Barcelona agreed to pay his medical expenses because they saw great potential in him. It is supposedly for this reason that Messi has always played for FC Barcelona.[40]

Friday's admiration for Messi perplexes his companions. In scene 8, the three discuss soccer:

> FRIDAY. ¿Juegas al fútbol?
> GABRIEL. ¿Yo? No.
> FRIDAY. Yo, sí. Y voy a ser como Messi.
> EMEKA. Más te valdría quitarte esas cosas de la cabeza.
> GABRIEL. ¿Por qué no como Eto'o? ¿O como Kanú, el más grande que ha dado Nigeria?
> FRIDAY. Porque ellos no vuelan. (Correa, *Friday*, 37–38)
>
> FRIDAY. Do you play soccer?
> GABRIEL. Me? No.
> FRIDAY. I do. And I'm going to be like Messi.
> EMEKA. It would be best for you to remove those thoughts from your head.
> GABRIEL. Why not like Eto'o? Or like Kanú, the greatest player Nigeria has had?
> FRIDAY. Because they don't fly.

The concept of an African boy not idolizing African players is inconceivable to Gabriel, but neither Eto'o nor Kanú have had the success of Messi, whose name is now synonymous with soccer greatness. On a subconscious level, this passage could be read in Fanonian terms as Friday attempting to approximate whiteness as a way to enter Europe. Friday's idolization of Messi has more to do with disability, however, as Messi overcame his disability to achieve global fame and admiration. Although Friday publicly denies his disability, his idolation of Messi suggests that, more so than identifying as African or Nigerian, he identifies as disabled, and seeks a disabled role model for himself. On the other hand, Friday's public denial of his disability and desire to be like the best (i.e., Messi) coincides with the notion that black athletes, through their bodies and talent, are perceived to transcend their race, a theme that also appears in Ozkar Galan's *Castigat ridendo mores* (2016) and Eva Hibernia's "La carrera" (unpublished manuscript).[41]

The ability to transcend race is a discursive ploy, a facade for capitalist exploitation of the black body. In his introduction to C. L. R. James's *Beyond a Boundary*, Robert Lipsyte notes that one could replace the soccer field in Nigeria for "any outpost of colonialism where a young man's only capital is his body. The exploitation is obvious, as is the hope. And, realistically, often the sheer lack of alternative opportunity."[42] This statement is powerful in articulating how race, migration, and sports intersect. An athlete of color holds value in contemporary Western society so long as his body is in top condition and submissive to the societal status quo, even at the expense of the athlete's dignity. Friday, having a limp and little athletic ability, is therefore dispensable. Furthermore, his lack of education, similar to the boy on whom his character is based, highlights that there is little that Spain can exploit from him.

Soccer is commonly known for being one of the world's most accessible sports because the only equipment required is a ball. Given the poverty of Friday's surroundings, it is logical for soccer to become his passion because, "cuando le doy a la pelota, estoy concentrado en eso y no pienso en otras cosas. No pienso en las amarillentas bolsas de los ojos de mi madre. Ni en mi tío. Es como si de repente se me apagara la cabeza y echara a volar" (when I kick the ball, I'm focused on that and I don't think about other things. I don't think about my mother's yellowing eye sockets. Nor about my uncle. It's as if suddenly my head turned off and took flight) (Correa, *Friday*, 35). Soccer, therefore, is a form of escapism through which Friday can truly be a child, without the stresses of the world. Friday is an embodiment of innocence and hope that ultimately are lost by the play's end.

The loss of innocence in the play can be broken down into six stages. The first is the death of Madre (Mother). Besides soccer, Friday's mother is his closest love; he skips school to be able to spend time with her and feed her, when he is not practicing. He is too young to understand how and why she got sick, but watching her die slowly affects him. Once she dies, there is no one left to convince him that he should stay in school, and as a result, soccer becomes his only goal. The second stage occurs when Tío sells the boys to a cacao farm in northern Nigeria. Olusegun tells his uncle: "Los que van se hacen viejos en dos años. No comen, trabajan hasta que les cruje la espalda. Algunos mueren" (Those who go become old in two years. They don't eat, they work until their backs crack. Some die) (42). Naively, Friday's only concern is whether he will have a pitch upon which to play soccer and if he will have a ball with which to practice. It is only when the boys are en route to the farm that he begins to comprehend why his brother was so adamant about not going there. The third stage occurs when the brothers are part of the pickpocketing ring in the port city. Although Friday is unaware of his role in the scheme, he witnesses Funto's mistreatment of his older brother. The fourth and fifth stages occur successively in scene 18, in which Friday is sexually assaulted by Oso, forced to perform a sexual act on him to receive passage to Europe. This violation leads to the melee in which Friday stabs Oso to death in an attempt to save his brother's life. The sixth stage occurs in scene 19 when Friday pushes Emeka off the boat because the latter bothers the former about his alleged inability to swim:

> EMEKA. Sí, ¡a nadar, chico, a nadar! Oh, pero ¿tú sabes nadar? No creo que sepas nadar. Ah no, tú no, tú solo nos vas a dar problemas. El maldito chico este. Y su balón.

> (*Friday se incorpora y empuja con violencia a Emeka. Oscuro. Un foco ilumina a Emeka. Se ahoga, lentamente. Vuelve la luz a Friday y Gabriel.*)

GABRIEL. Pero ¿por qué has hecho eso?
FRIDAY. Porque quería verle nadar. (84)

EMEKA. Yes, swim, kid, swim! Oh, but don't you know how to swim? I don't think you know how to swim. Ah no, not you, you are only going to give us problems. This damned kid. And his ball.

(*Friday stands up and violently pushes Emeka. Darkness. A light illuminates Emeka. He drowns, slowly. The light returns to Friday and Gabriel.*)

GABRIEL. But why did you do that?
FRIDAY. Because I wanted to see him swim.

Friday's frigid response could be read as lack of emotion and remorse, but given Emeka's incessant references to swimming, Friday simply may have wanted to see Emeka's skills, not realizing the consequences of his action.

Friday's fate as a tragic hero concludes at the end of scene 19 when Friday sees that "hay una pequeña luz que aparece y desaparece, aparece y desaparece, aparece y desaparece" (there is a small light that appears and disappears, appears and disappears, appears and disappears). He and Gabriel had finally reached the Entellada lighthouse on the island of Fuerteventura after a very long journey, but in that very moment, "*La pelota de trapo se escapa del regazo de Friday. Este se levanta y se va tras ella. Oscuro. Un foco ilumina a Friday. Gabriel grita su nombre, a lo lejos, mientras suena la sirena del barco. En el fondo del escenario aparece la luz de un faro*" (*The cloth ball escapes from Friday's lap. He stands up and goes after it. Darkness. A light shines on Friday. Gabriel shouts his name at a distance while the boat's horn sounds. In the stage's background appears the light of the lighthouse*) (84–85). Friday's death, a direct result of his desire to hold on to his most prized possession, only furthers to highlight his innocence. In the foreword to the play, playwright Itziar Pascual notes: "Friday es personaje y héroe trágico porque no está determinado al desastre, porque cree en la esperanza del cambio. No sería nunca posible lo trágico sin el fulgor de una esperanza que anima una libertad interior, esencial, profunda: la libertad del ser" (Friday is a character and tragic hero because he is not destined to disaster, because he believes in the hope of change. Tragedy would never be possible without the radiance of a hope that encourages an inner, essential, deep freedom: the freedom of the human being).[43] If the play were purely fiction, this statement would ring true, but the fact that the real-life Friday not only survived but also lives in Spain to this day problematizes the use of tragedy. Friday's death in the play ultimately strips him of humanity because his death is portrayed as predetermined because, as the prologue notes, death surrounds him from the opening of the play. His physical, social, and geographic circumstances circumscribe him within a circle of impossibility, made notable by Correa's designation of the play's end as "Fin (y principio)" (End [and beginning]) (Correa, *Friday*, 87). If the play is to be read as a circular narration, then Friday's death is the link that closes the circle, creating the soccer ball for which he searches.

Through the intersection of death, soccer, and innocence, *Friday* provides a necropolitical outlook into the relationship between Spain and Africa. The description of Nigeria as rampantly corrupt and dangerous (from environmental, medical, and physical standpoints) serves to portray Spain as a promised land for migrants, though the other two plays make clear that it is not. Friday's inability to reach Spain is tragic but also romanticized as he dies in search of his soccer ball. This romanticization is made clear in the final scene in which Friday, now dead, is able to fulfill his dream of being a professional soccer player:

> Y estoy ahí en medio, rodeado. No me tiembla ni un músculo. Espero. Empiezo a correr. Corro, corro, corro con el balón entre mis pies, y soy como un espíritu, porque todo lo que se me pone delante lo atravieso. Es como si no tuviera cuerpo. Como si pudiera ir a cualquier parte, porque nada ni nadie me lo impide. Soy como un suspiro de madre antes de morir. (87)
>
> And I'm there in the middle, surrounded. I don't tremble, not even a muscle. I wait. I start running. I run, run, run with the ball between my feet, and I'm like a spirit, because I go through everything put in front of me. It's as if I didn't have a body. As if I could go anywhere, because nothing and nobody can stop me. I'm like mother's sigh before dying.

In these final lines of the play, Friday repeats in the first person the monologue of scene 16 he recites in the third person in reference to Lionel Messi. This repetition allows Friday to become the next Messi in the afterlife, finally free from his disability, poverty, and other life circumstances. To end the play in this way not only portrays death as the only path to achieving one's dreams, but Friday's happiness in death also implies that life in Spain would never have brought him to such a state of euphoria.

It is worth questioning the purpose of creating a tragedy based on a story that does not end tragically. Friday's background serves to shed light on the poverty and desperation that lead him to migrate, but such stories are not new representations of Africa. The perspective of a disabled child surely does provoke sympathy, because from the moment he walks on stage, the spectator is aware that his dream of becoming the next Messi is next to impossible, but the real Friday is not disabled. The playwright's decision to portray Friday as disabled positions him on the least desirable level within each subgroup of his identity (black, African, Nigerian, male, child). Rather than inspire fear, as in the case of black, able-bodied adults discussed earlier in this chapter,

Friday is synonymous with the Western NGO (nongovernmental organization) perspective of Africa, which engenders pity. Therefore, it is his death that is used as a tool for understanding migration, similar to the case of Aylan Kurdi, the three-year-old Syrian boy whose lifeless body washed up on the shores of Turkey in September 2015, captured in a photo by Turkish press photographer Nilufer Demir. The rapid spread of the photo brought international awareness to the Syrian refugee crisis, the Syrian Civil War, and immigration to Europe. On a smaller scale, Correa's play has a similar objective, using death to bring awareness to the gravity of the migratory situation in Spain, underscoring and defying the systemic way society has become inured to black migrant deaths.

Do Black Lives Matter in Spain?

The three plays examined in this chapter align the conceptual symbolism presented by soccer, masculinity, death, and blackness, each contributing to the same necropolitical pattern that Spanish playwrights have maintained since the early 1990s. First, Ombasi, Jaro, and Friday all mention famous soccer players (Butragueño, Seerdorf, and Messi, respectively) as a cultural reference point to Spain. Given that soccer is Spain's most popular sport and one of its most powerful exports in terms of its national players and its teams that recruit considerable numbers of top players from other countries (e.g., FC Barcelona and Real Madrid), it is easy to understand why playwrights would use it as a point of reference. However, this then allows for a critique of the sports world and its role in promoting migration as a way for young children to achieve a better life. If there is a correlation between proximity to or aspiration for soccer and Spain, then all three characters would have at least demonstrated a willingness for cultural integration by participating in the national sport (in addition to other contributions they may bring). Their affinity for the sport, however, only serves to alert the spectator that there is some common knowledge between the Other and the self. This cultural cue ultimately gives false hope of cross-cultural interaction and empathy, just as it gives the three characters false hope of acceptance and integration.

Furthermore, the reference to soccer as a thread in all three plays brings into focus the role of black masculinity in Western sports. As Keith Nurse explains, "what remains problematic is that the fields of sport and entertainment are considered to emphasize body more than mind, and therefore recast Black masculinity within the traditional racialized, sexualized, infantilized and feminized framework."[44] This conceptualization of black masculinity is salient in the portrayal of Friday, who as a disabled child "athlete" is infantilized by making him younger than the real-life migrant and is simultaneously sexualized and feminized in the scene in which he is sexual assaulted by the smuggler kingpin. His naive dream of becoming a professional soccer player renders him vulnerable to adults manipulating him for their own personal interests.

In the case of Ombasi, his masculinity not only invokes sexual fear as discussed earlier in this chapter; he is also infantilized for not being able to communicate with the Spanish family since he only repeats two phrases in Spanish. Furthermore, his supposed athletic ability incites more fear as the Spanish family runs to their car to escape Ombasi and an impending storm in scene 12 because as La Madre declares desperately: "Nos va a coger. Corre más que nosotros. Todos los negros corren más. ¿No has visto las Olimpiadas?" (He's going to catch us. He runs faster than we do. All black people run faster. Haven't you seen the Olympics?)[45] This statement depicts black masculinity as formidable, ominous, and monstrous on a biological level, while also erasing any notion of black intellectual capacity.

The fact that Ombasi, Jaro, and Friday are male is a reflection of the national statistical data that shows that 65 percent of sub-Saharan migrants are male. This tendency toward focusing on male characters is also seen in cinema and prose. As previously mentioned, the image of the black man as a phobogenic object establishes a dynamic with Spanish characters that is not present in the plays that include black women, due to sexism and subjugation, as discussed in chapter 1 in relation to Afro-Caribbean women.

All three of these plays articulate a perspective in which black African migrants are incapable of establishing themselves in Spain. For example, the blackness of Ombasi, Jaro, and Friday is likened to pollution, symbolically justifying their deaths as a way to keep Spain "clean" from the stain of the Other. Death, whether by indifference, hatred, or blissful innocence, is a result of the national, transnational, and global political structures put in place to control migratory flows, which Robert Davidson terms interdiction, "the act of prohibiting, intercepting, or in some cases, deflecting unauthorized movement."[46] Interdiction, then, vis-à-vis African migrants, is the manifestation of necropolitical power present in these three plays, thereby demonstrating that black lives are, as Saidiya Hartman notes, "Imperiled and devalued by a racial calculus and a political arithmetic that were entrenched centuries ago."[47] In essence, black lives have not yet come to matter in Spain, because they represent an ultimate Other. As such, they are interdicted by individuals, groups, and even by geography. What hope is there for this situation to change or improve? From a theatrical standpoint, there has yet to be a Spanish immigration play that displays a story of black survival, wholly contradicting the existence of thousands of black Spaniards living in Spain today. The lack of positive stories about the lives of black migrants (or black Spaniards) maintains a necropolitical narrative that equates blackness with death.

Conclusion

✦

The Necropolitical Theater of Whiteness

Race and immigration intersect on the Spanish stage in ways that are surprisingly simple and consistent. The delineation of these patterns, as outlined in the previous three chapters, exposes the genealogy of a racial hierarchy rooted in prejudices that predate the large-scale immigration to Spain in the 1990s. The racial dynamics of immigration and citizenship in Spain impact the manner in which these nonwhite migrant groups have been portrayed on stage. The necropolitical hierarchy of race established in immigration theater conveys a dangerous message to the spectator: foreignness and nonwhiteness are antithetical to the Spanish state. The theatrical representation of all three groups discussed in this book establishes not simply a necropolitical theater but more specifically a necropolitical theater of whiteness, because ultimately these plays are meant for predominately white Spanish audiences, composed of spectators who have the ability to control and maintain the political and cultural structures that are in play. How are these theatrical patterns propagated and maintained? The necropolitical theater of whiteness is shaped by the following: a primary focus on nonwhite immigrants; bestowal of theatrical awards; plot devices that normalize whiteness as autochthonous; decriminalization or absolution of white criminality; didactic messages on how whiteness should operate; and finally, portrayals of white, able-bodied masculinity as constituting the top of the necropolitical hierarchy of race.

All Spanish immigration plays focus on nonwhite immigrants. If white immigrants appear at all, they are never central figures, as in the case of Ignacio del Moral's *Rey negro* (1997) or Fermín Cabal and Amanda Rodríguez's *Maldita cocina* (2007), in which Eastern European immigrants have small, secondary roles.[1] Although a considerable portion of the immigrant community in Spain is from other European nations such as Romania, Germany, and the United Kingdom, their whiteness protects them linguistically via the term "expat" and/or culturally through lack of artistic portrayals. This discrepancy bolsters what is presented in Spanish mass media, as immigration is always portrayed as a topic pertaining to nonwhite people through images of migrants in *pateras*, at border walls, or in detention centers. In this way, whiteness is normalized, even when it is foreign, thereby creating a problematic dynamic as there are now large numbers of nonwhite Spanish citizens who are continuously deemed "foreign," whereas thousands of white EU and Eastern European immigrants continue to enter the country and are welcomed, or at least not antagonized.

The vast majority of the plays discussed and analyzed in this book have been awarded national or local dramaturgy prizes. In fact, those that have not received awards, such as Fernando Martín Iniesta's *La falsa muerte de Jaro el negro*, have been plays that attempt to challenge whiteness or present cases of immigrant success, while still engaging in necropolitical tropes. As the juries of these theater awards are composed of other Spanish playwrights, many of whom have been awarded the same prizes for writing similar plays, a genealogy of plays that claim to humanize the immigration narrative is easily established through selection bias. This is in no way meant to disregard the artistic value or the quality of these plays but rather to critique the establishment of a canon based on repetitive themes of failure and death, which does little to humanize immigrants. If anything, these plays paint dark portrayals of the extreme, through which Spanish whiteness is unchallenged or even uplifted. Even in plays based on true stories, the necropolitical dynamic is used to further this "humanizing trope," as seen in Irma Correa's *Friday*.[2] Success for and vitality of nonwhite immigrants are not depicted, allowing spectators only to see the worst of the migratory experience rather than revealing to them possible experiences of real transcultural exchange that immigrants might undergo as they live their lives in Spain.

Portraying immigrants as inherently criminal or morally abject because of their decision to migrate or the choices they make upon arriving in Spain serves to shift criminality away from autochthonous Spaniards. In many of the plays discussed, white criminality is portrayed as absolvable or deemphasized in comparison with the purported criminality of the immigrant characters. For example, in Luis Araújo's *Mercado libre*, the lawyer is not only capable of hiding his own inhumane crimes but also tergiversates the evidence so as to get B's teenage sons off the hook for rape and gain them Spanish citizenship (symbolizing access to whiteness). The white actors' ability to unmask their neo-Nazi identities in the epilogue of *La falsa muerte de Jaro el Negro* absolves them (and the spectators) of their complicity in the murder they had just committed when in character. In Juan Pablo Heras's *Ataque preventivo*, the white characters' drug use fuels the drug trade that makes use of mules like Rachid necessary, yet he is portrayed as the criminal of the play. On the whole, immigrant characters serve as phobogenic agents, linked to criminality, thereby diminishing the importance of nonimmigrant characters' criminality or absolving them of it.

These plays not only teach us about national conceptualizations of immigrants but also that of Spaniards themselves. Autochthonous superiority is established through mythification of medieval figures from the Reconquista and more contemporary figures such as Francisco Franco. These figures, though polarizing, achieve the same result: yearning for homogeneity in response to burgeoning multiculturalism and diversity. Superiority is also established linguistically as in several plays immigrant characters are hyperbolically unable to speak Spanish well (e.g., Jaro in *La falsa muerte de Jaro el Negro*) or their variety of Spanish is portrayed as bastardized (e.g., Marisela in Carmen Resino's *Allegro* (*ma non troppo*) through purposeful misspellings in the text to indicate non-Castilian versions of Spanish.

Above all else, what is made alarmingly clear in all of these plays is that white Spanish men sit atop the necropolitical hierarchy of race. Although this is no surprise given the sociocultural dynamics of Western societies, it is striking given the alleged purpose of these plays: to highlight and humanize the immigrant experience. The only exception to this dynamic is when heteronormative norms are transgressed, as in the case of El Padre in Ignacio del Moral's *La mirada del hombre oscuro*. El Padre is punished not because of his ignorance or racism but rather because his form of masculinity does not uphold Spanish ideals of patriarchy. Unable to provide for his family physically, emotionally, or financially, El Padre is consequently upstaged by Ombasi, culminating in El Padre's loss of sight in one eye in the fight that takes place at the end of the play. This example demonstrates the racially gendered teachings that are transmitted via these works and how they operate vis-à-vis immigration.

All of these factors serve to establish a theater that stirs or calms autochthonous anxieties about the Other in the name of humanizing or sympathizing with the immigrant experience. Spanish necropolitical theater is built on a foundation of whiteness and patriarchy that seeps into how plays are written and performed (or not performed). As these tropes have evolved and solidified over the past three decades, one must question how the necropolitical theater can be dismantled. From a dramaturgical standpoint, my solution would be to create convivial theater, wherein racialized characters are depicted as part of the national fabric, while still approaching the possible outcomes of immigration: tolerance, integration, and identity negotiation.

My conceptualization of convivial theater is derived from Argentine philosopher Jorge Dubatti's notion of the *convivio*, which he describes as one of the three components of theater. According to Dubatti, "Llamamos convivio o acontecimiento convivial a la reunión, de cuerpo presente, sin intermediación tecnológica, de artistas, técnicos y espectadores en una encrucijada territorial cronotópica (unidad de tiempo y espacio) cotidiana (una sala, la calle, un bar, una casa, etc. en el tiempo presente)" (*Convivio*, or the convivial event, is what we call the meeting of artists, technicians, and spectators in the flesh, without technological mediation, at a quotidian [a theater, the street, a bar, a house, etc., in the present], chronotopic [a unit of time and space] territorial crossroads).[3] Later Dubatti writes, "En el teatro se vive con los otros: se establecen vínculos compartidos y vínculos vicarios que multiplican la afectación grupal" (In the theater, one lives with others: shared and vicarious links are established that cause the group affect to multiply) (62). This concept denotes not only the ephemeral and singular nature of theater but also its innately social character as it brings people together who, in theory, do not all know each other.

For me, Dubatti's conceptualization of the *convivio* takes on another semiotic dimension: that of how we can transcend Otherness via theater. In bringing together so many people for the purpose of a play about immigration, there is great affective potential for social change. However, the employment of necropolitical tropes works against theater's core mission: to allow us to live with others (*convivir* in Spanish). Therefore, in order for convivial theater to be possible, death should not be a central theme; instead, the process of living should be examined. Above all, such plays should challenge autochthonous characters on their prejudices, steer clear of sensationalized stereotypes, and promote the multicultural reality of Spain.

This is not to say that all works within convivial theater should be idyllic, for the reality of Spain is far from that. An example of a play that achieves many of the goals of convivial theater is Paco Bezerra's *El señor Ye ama los dragones* (2014).[4] This play not only has a diverse cast, having two Sino-Spanish actresses and two white Spanish actresses, but also makes Mandarin Chinese a central piece of the plot's development (translated for spectators via supertitles). It does not sugarcoat or exaggerate, as the play is based on the real Spanish phenomenon of nocturnal beer sales by Chinese migrants, and the conditions in which the characters live conveys a verisimilitude of the disparities between autochthonous and immigration communities.[5] At one point, the Sino-Spanish protagonist challenges her white Spanish counterparts on their use of racist jokes, and although one migrant character dies, her death is not used as a plot device for commentary on immigration. In this way, Bezerra's play can be seen as the bridge to a new canon of theater, one that delves into the lives of Spain's racialized citizens.

Now, nearly thirty years after the debut of *La mirada del hombre oscuro*, we must contemplate whether it is still worth creating plays about new arrivals, when the immigrants described in these plays have not only survived but now also have children, or even grandchildren, in Spain. The narrative shift toward understanding minority groups as citizens rather than immigrants, which is not meant to invalidate immigration, may facilitate an escape from the problematic, necropolitical constructions we have seen in Spanish theatrical production.

If theater's role in society is to push spectators to think about the world differently, then it comes at no benefit to promote sensationalized perspectives on immigration. For that, spectators could simply watch the local/national news. Instead, for Spanish theater to truly promote its national reality, it must do more to ensure that its playwrights, directors, technicians, and actors are trained to examine tough issues. As Isaias Fanlo and I have previously argued regarding the future of Catalan theater, theater academies must make a concerted effort to educate students on notions of race, ethnicity, and sexuality (all topics that are invisible or poorly represented on stage).[6] For this shift to be possible, however, theatrical curricula must be revamped to include required courses, or, at the very least, discussions, on race and ethnicity in Spain. This will not only create a more welcoming environment for racialized minorities who wish to enter the Spanish theater world but also prompt white students to reflect critically on how race is included in their theatricals works, whether they be actors, playwrights, directors, or technicians. In turn, we will likely see a new generation of plays that are more developed in terms of critical thinking about race, which will ultimately prompt spectators to have insightful conversations with those around them about Spain's present and future. As the nation continues to work out its relationship with migrants and citizens of color, convivial theater can provide a space through which these tensions can be explored and understood.

NOTES

Introduction

1. Inés D'Ors, "Léxico de la emigración," in *La inmigración en la literatura española contemporánea*, ed. Irene Andres-Suárez, Marco Kunz, and Inés D'Ors (Madrid: Verbum, 2002).

2. Other scholars analyze this phenomenon as well, including Désirée Kleiner-Liebau, *Migration and the Construction of National Identity in Spain* (Madrid: Iberoamericana, 2009).

3. For more on the rhetoric of autochthonous anxieties, see Jeffrey K. Coleman, "Autochthonous Anxieties, Immigration, and the Dangers of Demagoguery in Juan Diego Botto's 'Arquímedes,'" *Estreno* 44, no. 1 (2018): 71–89.

4. Ignacio del Moral, *La mirada del hombre oscuro* (Madrid: Fundación Autor, 1992); Concha Fernández Soto and Francisco Checa y Olmos, *Los mares de Caronte: Diecisiete calas dramáticas sobre migraciones* (Madrid: Fundamentos, 2016).

5. Baltasar Fra-Molinero, "The Suspect Whiteness of Spain," in *At Home and Abroad: Historicizing Twentieth-Century Whiteness in Literature and Performance*, ed. La Vinia Delois Jennings (Knoxville: University of Tennessee Press, 2009), 147; see also Susan Martin-Márquez, *Disorientations: Spanish Colonialism in Africa and the Performance of Identity* (New Haven, Conn.: Yale University Press, 2008).

6. Fra-Molinero, "The Suspect Whiteness of Spain," 153.

7. These two factors led me to omit the representation of Asian immigration from my analysis. Over the past decade, Chinese and Filipino migrants have grown to have a noticeable presence in Spain and are also racialized as nonwhite. There is a severe lack of Spanish theatrical work focusing on this community, however. The most notable Spanish theatrical work containing Asian protagonists is Paco Bezerra's 2014 play *El señor Ye ama los dragones* (Madrid: Instituto Nacional de las Artes Escénicas y la Música, 2014). This systemic invisibilization of Asian immigrants is necropolitical in and of itself.

8. J-A Mbembé and Libby Meintjes, "Necropolitics," *Public Culture* 15, no. 1 (2003): 11.

9. See chapter 1.

10. Lisa Marie Cacho, *Social Death: Racialized Rightlessness and the Criminalization of the Unprotected* (New York: New York University Press, 2012), 4.

11. Adrián Pérez-Melgosa, "Low-Intensity Necropolitics: Slow Violence and Migrant Bodies in Latin American Films," *Arizona Journal of Hispanic Cultural Studies* 20 (2016): 219.

12. Emma Cox, *Theatre and Migration* (London: Palgrave Macmillan, 2014), xii.

13. Eileen J. Doll, *Los inmigrantes en la escena española contemporánea: Buscando una nueva identidad española* (Madrid: Fundamentos, 2013).

14. Cox, *Theatre and Migration*, 22.
15. Pérez-Melgosa, "Low-Intensity Necropolitics," 219.
16. For more on Spanish emigration, see Raquel Vega-Durán, *Emigrant Dreams, Immigrant Borders: Migrants, Transnational Encounters, and Identity in Spain* (Lewisburg, Pa.: Bucknell University Press, 2016); Daniela Flesler, *The Return of the Moor: Spanish Responses to Contemporary Moroccan Immigration* (West Lafayette, Ind.: Purdue University Press, 2008); Jessica A. Folkart, *Liminal Fiction at the Edge of the Millennium: The Ends of Spanish Identity* (Lewisburg, Pa.: Bucknell University Press, 2014); Benita Sampedro Vizcaya and Simon R. Doubleday, *Border Interrogations: Questioning Spanish Frontiers* (New York: Berghahn Books, 2008); Irene Andres-Suárez, Marco Kunz, and Inés D'Ors, *La inmigración en la literatura española contemporánea* (Madrid: Verbum, 2002).
17. Álvaro Rengifo Calderón and Antonio Oporto del Olmo, "Historia, presente y prospectiva de las migraciones en España," *Información Comercial Española* 826 (2005): 159.
18. Ruben Andersson, *Illegality, Inc.: Clandestine Migration and the Business of Bordering Europe* (Oakland: University of California Press, 2014), 20.
19. "Ley Orgánica 7/1985, de 1 de julio, sobre derechos y libertades de los extranjeros en España," *Boletín Oficial del Estado* 158 (July 3, 1985): 20824.
20. For more information on the history of *pateras* and their interception, see Guillaume Le Boedec, "Le détroit de Gibraltar: Les limites d'un espace modèle de la lutte européenne contre les migrations irrégulières," *EchoGéo* 2 (2007), https://doi.org/10.4000/echogeo.1488, http://journals.openedition.org/echogeo/1488.
21. Frantz Fanon, *Black Skin, White Masks* (New York: Grove Press, 2008 [first published in French in 1952 by Éditions Seuil]), 129.
22. Antonio M. Bañón Hernández, *Discurso e inmigración: Propuestas para el análisis de un debate social* (Murcia, Spain: Universidad de Murcia, 2002).
23. Teun A. van Dijk, *Racism and Discourse in Spain and Latin America*, Discourse Approaches to Politics, Society, and Culture (Amsterdam: John Benjamins, 2005), 37.
24. David Moffette, *Governing Irregular Migration: Bordering Culture, Labour, and Security in Spain* (Vancouver: UBC Press, 2018), 12.
25. Moffette, *Governing Irregular Migration*, 3–4.
26. Andersson, *Illegality, Inc.*, 1.
27. Moffette, *Governing Irregular Migration*, 100–108.
28. Parvati Nair, "Europe's 'Last' Wall: Contiguity, Exchange, and Heterotopia in Ceuta, the Confluence of Spain and North Africa," in *Border Interrogations: Questioning Spanish Frontiers*, ed. Benita Sampedro Vizcaya and Simon Doubleday (New York: Bergahn Books, 2008), 15–41.
29. Henk Driessen, "The 'New Immigration' and the Transformation of the European-African Border," in *Border Identities: Nation and State at International Frontiers*, ed. Thomas Wilson and Hastings Donnan (Cambridge: Cambridge University Press, 1998), 96.
30. For the complete INE data, see Instituto Nacional de Estadística, "Saldo migratorio con el extranjero por año, país de nacimiento y nacionalidad (española/extranjera)," http://www.ine.es/jaxiT3/Tabla.htm?t=24310&L=0.

31. Susanne Zantop, *Colonial Fantasies: Conquest, Family, and Nation in Precolonial Germany, 1770–1870* (Durham, N.C.: Duke University Press, 1997), vii.

32. This phrase harkens back to the protest slogan used in the United Kingdom in the 1970s and 1980s by black and Asian antiracism activists.

33. There are two explanations for this discrepancy. First, as Spanish women joined the national labor force in the 1980s and 1990s, gender roles regarding the home did not shift in accordance and therefore there was a void that could be filled by foreign domestic workers. Second, beginning in 1993, a labor quota system was established to give work visas to immigrants, within which there was a preference for domestic service workers, particularly from those who already spoke Spanish.

34. These stereotypes are not limited to theater, as demonstrated in the depiction of Latin American women in films such as Fernando León de Aranoa's *Princesas* (2005) and Icíar Bollaín's *Flores de otro mundo* (1999), among others.

35. See Ricard Zapata-Barrero, "The Muslim Community and Spanish Tradition: Maurophobia as a Fact, and Impartiality as a Desideratum," in *Multiculturalism, Muslims and Citizenship: A European Approach*, ed. Tariq Modood, Anna Triandafyllidou, and Ricard Zapata-Barrero (New York: Routledge, 2006). Other studies that explore the cultural dynamics between Morocco and Spain are Susan Martin-Márquez's *Disorientations*, Daniela Flesler's *Return of the Moor*, and the final chapter of Jessica Folkart's *Liminal Fiction*.

Chapter 1

1. A translation of this section of the law was provided in the introduction.

2. Ruben Andersson, *Illegality, Inc.: Clandestine Migration and the Business of Bordering Europe* (Oakland: University of California Press, 2014), 21.

3. David Moffette, *Governing Irregular Migration: Bordering Culture, Labour, and Security in Spain* (Vancouver: UBC Press, 2018), 45.

4. Moffette, *Governing Irregular Migration*, 45n27.

5. Gabriel García Márquez, "Señor presidente," *El País* (Madrid), March 18, 2001, España, https://elpais.com/diario/2001/03/18/espana/984870010_850215.html.

6. García Márquez, "Señor presidente."

7. Vicente Torrado, "La inmigración latinoamericana en España," *Departamento de Asuntos Económicos y Sociales. Organización de las Naciones Unidas* (2006): 2.

8. Enakshi Dua, "Exclusion through Inclusion: Female Asian Migration in the Making of Canada as a White Settler Nation," *Gender, Place and Culture* 14, no. 4 (2007): 446.

9. Antonio Izquierdo Escribano and Raquel Martínez-Buján, "From Favourites to 'With No Return': Permanence and Mobility of Latin American Immigration in Spain during the 21st Century," *Canadian Ethnic Studies* 46, no. 3 (2014): 109.

10. Alberto de Casso Basterrechea, *Los viernes del Hotel Luna Caribe* (*LVHLC*), in *Primer acto* 283 (2000): 87. Subsequent in-text page references for *LVHLC* refer to this source.

11. Nancy Morejón, *Looking Within: Selected Poems, 1954–2000*, ed. Juanamaría Cordones-Cook, trans. Gabriel Abudu et al. (Detroit: Wayne State University Press, 2003), 236–37.

12. Neil Roberts, *Freedom as Marronage* (Chicago: University of Chicago Press, 2015), 13.

13. Luis Araújo, *Mercado libre* (*ML*) (Madrid: Asociación de Autores de Teatro, 2008), 16.

14. Luis Foronda, "'Mercado libre' o las enfermedades del espíritu humano," in *ML*, ed. Luis Araújo (Bilbao, Spain: Artezblai, 2008), 13.

15. Antonio Daniel García Orellana, "Eco," in *ML*, 6–7.

16. García Orellana, "Eco," 9.

17. José Monleón, "Prólogo," in *ML*, 11.

18. There are no stage directions to clarify the setting of scene 15.

19. Monleón, "Prólogo," 11.

20. I take this tendency to be a vestige of Spanish colonialism. It is for this reason that Filipina and Latin American women tend to be seen as better caretakers and nannies than black and Arab women.

21. Carmen Resino, *Unos pájaros verdes* (*UPV*), in *Los mares de Caronte: Diecisiete calas dramáticas sobre migraciones*, ed. Concha Fernández Soto and Francisco Checa y Olmos (Madrid: Fundamentos, 2016), 211.

22. Désirée Kleiner-Liebau, *Migration and the Construction of National Identity in Spain* (Madrid: Iberoamericana, 2009), 80.

23. The use of the word *jornada* instead of *acto* can be interpreted as a way to privilege Marisela's protagonism, which also zeros in on her social position as a maid.

24. Luisa García-Manso, "Género e inmigración en el teatro español contemporáneo: *Allegro (Ma non troppo)* de Carmen Resino," *Estreno* 37, no. 1 (2011): 74.

25. Carmen Resino, *Allegro (ma non troppo)* (*AMNT*), in *Teatro con múscia* (Madrid: Fundamentos, 2008), 169.

26. García-Manso, "Género e inmigración en el teatro español contemporáneo," 79.

27. Catherine B. Ross, "¡Mami, qué buena estás! Representations of the Immigrant Woman in 'Sobreviviré' (1999) and 'I Love You Baby' (2001)," *Letras Femeninas* 34, no. 1 (2008): 227.

Chapter 2

1. It is worth noting that the word *raza* in Spanish was originally used for animals in the sense of "breed" or "species," but morphed in the medieval era into "race" as we commonly know it now, thus connoting an animalistic view of otherness that has remained constant until today.

2. Ministerio de Empleo y Seguridad Social (Ministry of Employment and Social Security), Observatorio Permanente de la Inmigración (Permanent Immigration Observatory), *Extranjeros residentes en España: A 30 de junio de 2016* (2016), table T1, 4.

3. Bernabé López, "La inmgración de magrebíes y africanos: Asumir la vecindad," in *De la España que emigra a la España que acoge*, ed. A. A. Vigil et al. (Madrid: Fundación Francisco Largo Caballero, 2006), 485.

4. López, "La inmgración de magrebíes y africanos," 485–86.

5. Xavier Rius Sant, *El libro de la inmigración en España*, 1st ed., Pensamiento político, Temas de actualidad (Córdoba, Spain: Almuzara, 2007), 201.

6. For a deeper explanation of how the truth of the attack was manipulated in the Spanish press and later rectified, see Jesús Cebrerio's erratum in *El País*. Jesús Cebrerio, "A propósito de mentiras," *El País* (Madrid), March 27, 2004, https://elpais.com/diario/2004/03/27/espana/1080342027_850215.html.

7. David Moffette, *Governing Irregular Migration: Bordering Culture, Labour, and Security in Spain* (Vancouver: UBC Press, 2018), 55.

8. "Seven Theses on Today's Terrorism," updated September 21, 2004, www3.georgetown.edu/president/aznar/inauguraladdress.html.

9. Ricard Zapata-Barrero, "The Muslim Community and Spanish Tradition: Maurophobia as a Fact, and Impartiality as a Desideratum," in *Multiculturalism, Muslims and Citizenship: A European Approach*, ed. Tariq Modood, Anna Triandafyllidou, and Ricard Zapata-Barrero (New York: Routledge, 2006), 144.

10. Moffette, *Governing Irregular Migration*, 70.

11. Moffette, 70–71; Mae M. Ngai, *Impossible Subjects: Illegal Aliens and the Making of Modern America* (Princeton, N.J.: Princeton University Press, 2004).

12. Daniela Flesler, *The Return of the Moor: Spanish Responses to Contemporary Moroccan Immigration* (West Lafayette, Ind.: Purdue University Press, 2008), 3.

13. Susan Martin-Márquez, *Disorientations: Spanish Colonialism in Africa and the Performance of Identity* (New Haven, Conn.: Yale University Press, 2008), 8–9.

14. López, "La inmgración de magrebíes y africanos," 475.

15. Other plays about North African immigration include *La orilla rica* by Encarna de las Heras (Madrid: Centro Nacional de Nuevas Tendencias Escénicas, 1994), *Amanecer en Orán* by Ignasi García i Barba (Valladolid, Spain: Caja España, 1996), *Oasi* by Carles Batlle (Barcelona: Edicions 62, 2003), *Memoria fotográfica* by Beth Escudé i Gallès (Madrid: Fundamentos, 2006), *Temptació* by Carles Batlle (Barcelona: Proa, 2004), *Despedida* by Raúl Hernández Garrido (Madrid: Fundación Autor, 2006), *Entrevías* by Yolanda Pallín (Madrid: Fundación Autor, 2006), *Fútbol* by Pedro Casablanc (León, Spain: Caja España, 2008), and *Zahra, favorita de Al-Andalus* by Antonia Bueno Mingallón (Cáceras, Spain: Universidad de Extremadura, 2009).

16. Flesler, *Return of the Moor*, 5.

17. Marco Kunz, "El drama de la inmigración: *La mirada del hombre oscuro* de Ignacio del Moral y *Ahlán* de Jerónimo López Mozo," in *La inmigración en la literatura española contemporánea*, ed. Irene Andres-Suárez, Marco Kunz, and Inés D'Ors (Madrid: Verbum, 2002), 233–34.

18. Jerónimo López Mozo, *Ahlán* (Oviedo, Spain: KRK, 2010), 53.

19. López Mozo, *Ahlán*, 53–54.

20. See Parvati Nair, "Europe's 'Last' Wall: Contiguity, Exchange, and Heterotopia in Ceuta, the Confluence of Spain and North Africa," in *Border Interrogations: Questioning Spanish Frontiers*, ed. Benita Sampedro Vizcaya and Simon Doubleday (New York: Bergahn Books, 2008), 15–41.

21. Etienne Balibar and Immanuel Maurice Wallerstein, *Race, Nation, Class: Ambiguous Identities* (London: Verso, 1991), 17–18.

22. Kunz, "El drama de la inmigración," 238.

23. Kunz, "El drama de la inmigración," 247–48.

24. Flesler, *Return of the Moor*, 10.

25. Flesler, *Return of the Moor*, 21.

26. Juan Goytisolo, *Paisajes después de la batalla* (Barcelona: Montesinos, 1982).

27. Although the play debuted in both Spanish and English in 1997, its text was only published in English by the Royal Court Theatre. In addition, Planell updated the play in 2014 in Spanish for new audiences. For consistency, however, I will be citing from the 1997 original English text of the play.

28. David Planell, *Bazaar*, in *Spanish Plays: New Spanish and Catalan Drama*, ed. Elyse Dodgson and Mary Peate (London: Nick Hern Books, 1999), 131–32.

29. *National Security Strategy of the United States of America* (Washington, D.C., 2002).

30. Juan Pablo Heras, *Ataque preventivo (puzzle dramático en 31 piezas para 6/8 actores)* (Madrid: Asociación de Autores de Teatro: Consejería de Cultura de la Comunidad de Madrid, 2005), 16–17.

31. Hugo Salcedo, *El viaje de los cantores* (Toluca: Universidad Autónoma del Estado de México, 2014). This play was awarded Spain's prestigious Tirso de Molina Theater Prize in 1989.

32. For more information about the events that inspired Salcedo's play, see the press release "Tráfico humano: 18 mexicanos muertos al intentar pasar a E.U.," *La Jornada*, July 3, 1987, 1.

33. Salcedo, *El viaje de los cantores*, 29–30.

34. Lewis R. Gordon, *Existentia Africana: Understanding Africana Existential Thought* (New York: Routledge, 2000), 69.

35. Flesler, *Return of the Moor*, 4.

Chapter 3

1. Other plays that portray sub-Saharan African migration are Ignacio del Moral's *Rey Negro* (Guadalajara, Spain: Ezcurra, 1997); Alberto Miralles's *Mongo, Boso, Rosco, N'Goe . . . Oniyá*, in *Teatro breve 2* (Madrid: Fundamentos, 1999), 95–109; Borja Ortiz de Gondra's *Mane, Thecel, Phares* (Lleida, Spain: Universitat de Lleida, 2000); José Moreno Arenas's *El aparcamiento*, in *Trilogías indigestas [I]* (Salobreña, Spain: Alhulia-La Avispa, 2004), 163–84; Malco Arija Martínez's *Akua, perdida en el tiempo, in Teatro Promoción 1998–2002* (Madrid: Fundamentos, 2003), 13–73; Juan Diego Botto and Roberto Cossa's *El privilegio de ser perro* (Barcelona: El Aleph, 2005); Josep Pere Peyró's *La tanca*, in *Estudis escènics 36* (2009): 398–408; Jerónimo López Mozo's *La verdad de los sueños*, in *Obras galardonadas en el V Concurso Iberoamericano de Dramaturgia Infantil*, ed. Jerónimo López Mozo, Jesús del Castillo, and Maxi Rodríguez (Bilbao, Spain: Centro de Documentación de las Artes de los Títeres de Bilbao, 2010), 11–44; Juana Escabias's *Tu sangre sobre la arena*, in *Literatura Española desde 1939 hasta la actualidad,* ed. Francisco Gutiérrez Carbajo (Madrid: Editorial Universitaria Ramón Areces-UNED, 2011), 285–87; Mar Gómez Glez's *Cifras* (Madrid: Centro de Documentación Teatral, 2012); Juan Diego Botto's *Invisibles: Voces de "Un Trozo invisible de este mundo"* (Barcelona: Espasa, 2013); and Ozkar Galán's *Castigat ridendo mores*, in *Los mares de Caronte: Diecisiete calas dramáticas sobre migraciones*, ed. Concha Fernández Soto and Francisco Checa y Olmos (Madrid: Fundamentos, 2016), 135–49.

2. See Nick Jones, "Cosmetic Ontologies, Cosmetic Subversions: Articulating Black Beauty and Humanity in Luis de Góngora's 'En la fiesta del Santísimo Sacramento,'" *Journal for Early Modern Cultural Studies* 15, no. 1 (2015): 26–54.

3. See Helen Graham and Antonio Sánchez, "The Politics of 1992," in *Spanish Cultural Studies: An Introduction*, ed. Jo Labanyi and Helen Graham (Oxford: Oxford University Press, 1995), 406–18.

4. Marco Kunz, "El drama de la inmigración: *La mirada del hombre oscuro* de Ignacio del Moral y *Ahlán* de Jerónimo López Mozo," in *La Inmigración En La Literatura Española Contemporánea*, ed. Irene Andres-Suárez, Marco Kunz, and Inés D'Ors (Madrid: Verbum, 2002), 216.

5. Bernabé López, "La inmgración de magrebíes y africanos: Asumir la vecindad," in *De la España que emigra a la España que acoge*, ed. A. A. Vigil, A. Asenjo, M. J. Aguilar, and Caballero Fundación Francisco Largo (Madrid: Fundación Francisco Largo Caballero, 2006), 482.

6. Isabella Alexander, "The Crossing," GlobalPost Investigations, PRI (Public Radio International) (2016), https://gpinvestigations.pri.org/the-crossing-eb527318eb76.

7. Alexander, "The Crossing."

8. "Dentro de esta línea merece destacarse la preocupación de la Ley por un tratamiento preferencial en favor de los iberoamericanos, portugueses, filipinos, andorranos, ecuatoguineanos, sefardíes y de los originarios de la ciudad de Gibraltar, por darse en ellos los supuestos de identidad o afinidad cultural que les hacen acreedores a esta consideración" ("Ley Orgánica 7/1985," 20824).

9. López, "La inmgración de magrebíes y africanos," 487.

10. Antumi Toasije, "The Africanity of Spain: Identity and Problematization," *Journal of Black Studies* 39, no. 3 (2009): 351.

11. In the English translation, Ombasi names Sánchez-Vícario, another famed player of Real Madrid. Ignacio del Moral, *La mirada del hombre oscuro* (Madrid: Fundación Autor, 1992), 24.

12. del Moral, *La mirada del hombre oscuro*, 17; Ignacio del Moral, *Dark Man's gaze (La mirada del hombre oscuro); A Mommy and a Daddy (Papis); Little Bears (Oseznos)*, trans. Jartu Gallashaw Toles (New Brunswick, N.J.: Estreno Plays, 2005), 3.

13. del Moral, *Dark Man's Gaze*, 5.

14. Etienne Balibar and Immanuel Maurice Wallerstein, *Race, Nation, Class: Ambiguous Identities* (London: Verso, 1991), 17.

15. Frantz Fanon, *Black Skin, White Masks* (New York: Grove Press, 2008 [first published in French in 1952 by Éditions Seuil]), 129.

16. Camilla Stevens, "Encuentros culturales: La parodia postcolonialista en *La isla amarilla* y *La mirada del hombre oscuro*," in *Entre actos: Diálogos sobre teatro español entre siglos*, ed. Martha T. Halsey and Phyllis Zatlin (University Park, Pa.: Estreno Plays, 1999), 183.

17. See Fernando Martin Iniesta's *La falsa muerte de Jaro el negro*, discussed later in this chapter, and Juan Diego Botto's monologue, "Arquímedes," found in *Invisibles*.

18. Graham and Sánchez, "The Politics of 1992," 415.

19. Toasije, "The Africanity of Spain," 350.

20. del Moral, *La mirada del hombre oscuro*, 96.

21. del Moral, *Dark Man's Gaze*, 38.

22. This concept of traversing a border to reach Europe is made literal in Ozkar Galán's *Castigat ridendo mores*, in which an African is challenged to cross a red

line in the sand that will him allow to officially enter into Europe. For more information on the conceptualization of immigration literature as liminal fiction, see Jessica A. Folkart, *Liminal Fiction at the Edge of the Millennium: The Ends of Spanish Identity* (Lewisburg, Pa.: Bucknell University Press, 2014).

23. This play has never been staged. In addition, as Eileen J. Doll notes, the publication of this play in both traditional and children's theater collections has created ambiguity as to what Martín Iniesta's ideal audience would be for this play. Eileen J. Doll, *Los inmigrantes en la escena española contemporánea: Buscando una nueva identidad Española* (Madrid: Fundamentos, 2013), 235.

24. Fernando Martín Iniesta, "La falsa muerte de Jaro el Negro," in *Teatro breve entre dos siglos*, ed. Virtudes Serrano (Madrid: Cátedra, 2004), 132.

25. Esteban Ibarra, *Los crímenes del odio: Violencia skin y neonazi en España* (Madrid: Ediciones Temas de Hoy, 2003), 46.

26. Rafael García Serrano, *Eugenio o Proclamación de la Primavera* (Madrid: Jerarquía, 1938).

27. Eugenio G. de Nora, *La novela española contemporánea (1939–1967)* (Madrid: Gredos, 1970), 43.

28. Balibar and Wallerstein, *Race, Nation, Class*, 37.

29. The concept of *unidad de destino* was articulated by José Antonio Primo de Rivera in his 1933 speech entitled "Puntos Iniciales." José Antonio Primo de Rivera, "Puntos iniciales," *FE* (1933).

30. Ibarra, *Los crímenes del odio*, 33.

31. Christina Sharpe, *In the Wake: On Blackness and Being* (Durham, N.C.: Duke University Press, 2016), 15.

32. Bernard Beckerman, *Dynamics of Drama: Theory and Method of Analysis* (New York: Knopf, 1970), 149.

33. Susan Sontag, *Regarding the Pain of Others* (New York: Farrar, Straus and Giroux, 2003), 102.

34. Jacinto Benavente, *Los intereses creados*, ed. Fernando Lázaro Carreter (Madrid: Cátedra, 1974); Pedro Calderón de la Barca, *El gran teatro del mundo / El gran mercado del mundo*, ed. Eugenio Frutos Cortés (Madrid: Cátedra, 1974).

35. One example of this is the Museo Atlántico, an underwater museum off the coast of Lanzarote composed of twelve sculpture installations with more than three hundred life-size figures meant to symbolize the many migrants who have died in those waters.

36. This play has not yet been staged for two reasons. First, the play requires five black actors, including one child to play Friday, which according to the playwright has not been achievable in Spain. Second, plays with larger casts are often too expensive to stage in the current economic conditions of the Spanish theater world. As a result, Correa is currently having the play translated into English so that it may be staged in the United Kingdom or the United States.

37. See Juan Diego Botto's 2005 monologue "La carta," a fictionalized account of the deaths of Yaguine Koita and Fodé Tounkara, who in 1999 froze to death while stowed away in the wheel well of a Sabena Airlines flight from Conakry to Brussels. Juan Diego Botto, "La carta," in *El privilegio de ser perro*.

38. Juan Manuel Pardellas, "El niño polizón que sueña con Messi," *El País* (Madrid), November 17, 2007, España, 21.

39. Irma Correa, *Friday* (Madrid: Fundación Autor, 2011), 22.

40. See Guillem Balagué, *Messi* (London: Orion, 2014).

41. Ozkar Galán, "Castigat ridendo mores"; Eva Hibernia, "La Carrera." Unpublished manuscript, last modified October 17, 2017. PDF file.

42. Robert Lipsyte, introduction to *Beyond a Boundary: 50th Anniversary Edition*, ed. C. L. R. James (Durham, N.C.: Duke University Press, 2013), xvii.

43. Itziar Pascual, "Un aliento de djembé," in *Friday*, ed. Irma Correa (Madrid: Fundación Autor, 2011), 8.

44. Keith Nurse, "Masculinities in Transition: Gender and the Global Problematique," in *Interrogating Caribbean Masculinities: Theoretical and Empirical Analyses*, ed. Rhoda E. Reddock (Kingston, Jamaica: University of the West Indies Press, 2004), 31.

45. del Moral, *La mirada del hombre oscuro*, 86; del Moral, *Dark Man's Gaze*, 33.

46. Robert A. Davidson, "Introduction: Spaces of Immigration 'Prevention': Interdiction and the Nonplace," *Diacritics* 33, no. 3 (2003): 5.

47. Saidiya Hartman, *Lose Your Mother: A Journey along the Atlantic Slave Route* (New York: Farrar, Straus, and Giroux, 2007), 6.

Conclusion

1. Ignacio del Moral, *Rey negro* (Guadalajara, Spain: Ezcurra, 1997); Fermín Cabal and Amanda Rodríguez, *Maldita cocina*, in *Caballito del diablo / Maldita cocina*, ed. Fermín Cabal (León, Spain: Edilesa, 2007), 69–135.

2. See chapter 3.

3. Jorge Dubatti, "Filosofía del Teatro: Fundamentos y corolarios," *Gestos* 25, no. 50 (2010): 61.

4. For a more in-depth analysis of this play, see Jeffrey K. Coleman, "Privileging the Oriental in Paco Bezerra's *El señor Ye ama los dragones*," *Symposium: A Quarterly Journal in Modern Literatures* 72, no. 1 (2018): 3–12.

5. The *lateros* (can sellers) sell beer and soda by the can illegally in the streets and plazas of Madrid. This market is dominated by Chinese migrants, but other migrant groups are involved as well. According to an investigative report, the fine for selling cans ranges from €150 to €1,200. For more on this, see Ana Iris Simón, "Pasé una noche con los lateros del centro de Madrid," *Vice*, August 15, 2017, https://www.vice.com/es/article/599pdb/noche-lateros-madrid.

6. See Jeffrey K. Coleman and Isaías Fanlo, "Els invisibles i els silenciats: Algunes reflexions epistolars sobre qüestions racials i queer en el teatre català," *Pausa* 40 (2018), http://www.revistapausa.cat/els-invisibles-i-els-silenciats-algunes-reflexions-epistolars-sobre-questions-racials-i-queer-en-el-teatre-catala.

BIBLIOGRAPHY

Alexandra, Isabella. "The Crossing." GlobalPost Investigations, PRI (Public Radio International), 2016. https://gpinvestigations.pri.org/the-crossing-eb527318eb76.

Andersson, Ruben. *Illegality, Inc.: Clandestine Migration and the Business of Bordering Europe*. Oakland: University of California Press, 2014.

Andres-Suárez, Irene, Marco Kunz, and Inés d'Ors. *La inmigración en la literatura española contemporánea*. Madrid: Verbum, 2002.

Araújo, Luis. *Mercado libre*. Madrid: Asociación de Autores de Teatro, 2008.

Arija Martínez, Malco. *Akua, perdida en el tiempo*. In *Teatro: Promoción 1998–2002*, 13–73. Madrid: Editoria; Fundamentos, 2003.

Balagué, Guillem. *Messi*. London: Orion, 2014.

Balibar, Etienne, and Immanuel Maurice Wallerstein. *Race, Nation, Class: Ambiguous Identities*. London: Verso, 1991.

Bañón Hernández, Antonio M. *Discurso e inmigración: Propuestas para el análisis de un debate social*. Murcia, Spain: Universidad de Murcia, 2002.

Batlle, Carles. *Oasi*. Barcelona: Edicions 62, 2003.

———. *Temptació*. Barcelona: Proa, 2004.

Beckerman, Bernard. *Dynamics of Drama: Theory and Method of Analysis*. New York: Knopf, 1970.

Benavente, Jacinto. *Los intereses creados*. Edited by Fernando Lázaro Carreter. Madrid: Cátedra, 1974.

Botto, Juan Diego. "La Carta." In *El privilegio de ser perro*, edited by Juan Diego Botto and Roberto Cossa, 39–52. Barcelona: El Aleph, 2005.

———. *Invisibles: Voces de "Un Trozo invisible de este mundo."* Barcelona: Espasa, 2013.

Bueno Mingallón, Antonia. *Zahra, favorita de Al-Andalus*. Cáceres, Spain: Universidad de Extremadura, 2009.

Cabal, Fermín, and Amanda Rodríguez. *Maldita cocina*. In *Caballito del diablo / Maldita cocina*. Edited by Fermín Cabal, 69–135. León, Spain: Edilesa, 2007.

Cacho, Lisa Marie. *Social Death: Racialized Rightlessness and the Criminalization of the Unprotected*. New York: New York University Press, 2012.

Calderón de la Barca, Pedro. *El gran teatro del mundo / El gran mercado del mundo*. Edited by Eugenio Frutos Cortés. Madrid: Cátedra, 1974.

Casablanc, Pedro. *Fútbol*. León, Spain: Caja España, 2008.

Cebrerio, Jesús. "A propósito de mentiras." *El País* (Madrid), March 27, 2004. https://elpais.com/diario/2004/03/27/espana/1080342027_850215.html.

Coleman, Jeffrey K. "Autochthonous Anxieties, Immigration, and the Dangers of Demagoguery in Juan Diego Botto's *Arquímedes*." *Estreno* 44, no. 1 (2018): 71–89.

———. “Privileging the Oriental in Paco Bezerra’s *El Señor Ye Ama Los Dragones.*” *Symposium: A Quarterly Journal in Modern Literatures* 72, no. 1 (2018): 3–12.

Coleman, Jeffrey K., and Isaías Fanlo. “Els invisibles i els silenciats: Algunes reflexions epistolars sobre qüestions racials i queer en el teatre català.” *Pausa* 40 (2018). http://www.revistapausa.cat/els-invisibles-i-els-silenciats-algunes-reflexions-epistolars-sobre-questions-racials-i-queer-en-el-teatre-catala.

Correa, Irma. *Friday.* Madrid: Fundación Autor, 2011.

Cox, Emma. *Theatre and Migration.* London: Palgrave Macmillan, 2014.

Davidson, Robert A. “Introduction: Spaces of Immigration ‘Prevention’: Interdiction and the Nonplace.” *Diacritics* 33, no. 3 (2003): 3–18.

de Casso Basterrechea, Alberto. *Los viernes del hotel luna caribe.* In *Primer acto* 283 (2000): 65–113.

de las Heras, Encarna. *La orilla rica.* Madrid: Centro Nacional de Nuevas Tendencias Escénicas, 1994.

del Moral, Ignacio. *Dark Man’s Gaze (La mirada del hombre oscuro); A Mommy and a Daddy (Papis); Little Bears (Oseznos).* Translated by Jartu Gallashaw Toles. New Brunswick, N.J.: Estreno Plays, 2005.

———. *La mirada del hombre oscuro.* Madrid: Fundación Autor, 1992.

———. *Rey negro.* Guadalajara, Spain: Ezcurra, 1997.

de Nora, Eugenio G. *La novela española contemporánea (1939–1967).* Madrid: Gredos, 1970.

Dijk, Teun A. van. *Racism and Discourse in Spain and Latin America.* Discourse Approaches to Politics, Society, and Culture. Amsterdam: John Benjamins, 2005.

Doll, Eileen J. *Los inmigrantes en la escena española contemporánea: Buscando una nueva identidad española.* Madrid: Fundamentos, 2013.

D’Ors, Inés. “Léxico de la emigración.” In *La inmigración en la literatura española contemporánea*, edited by Irene Andres-Suárez, Marco Kunz, and Inés D’Ors, 21–108. Madrid: Verbum, 2002.

Driessen, Henk. “The ‘New Immigration’ and the Transformation of the European-African Border.” In *Border Identities: Nation and State at International Frontiers*, edited by Thomas Wilson and Hastings Donnan, 96–116. Cambridge: Cambridge University Press, 1998.

Dua, Enakshi. “Exclusion through Inclusion: Female Asian Migration in the Making of Canada as a White Settler Nation.” *Gender, Place and Culture* 14, no. 4 (2007): 445–66.

Dubatti, Jorge. “Filosofía Del Teatro: Fundamentos Y Corolarios.” *Gestos* 25, no. 50 (2010): 53–81.

Escabias, Juana. *Tu sangre sobre la arena.* In *Literatura española desde 1939 hasta la actualidad*, edited by Francisco Gutiérrez Carbajo, 285–87. Madrid: Editorial Universitaria Ramón Areces-UNED, 2011.

Escudé i Gallès, Beth. *Memoria fotográfica.* In *Mujeres sobre mujeres en los albores del siglo XXI: Teatro breve español = One-act Spanish Plays by Women about Women in the Early Years of the 21st Century*, edited by Patricia W. O’Connor, 287–300. Madrid: Fundamentos, 2006.

Fanon, Frantz. *Black Skin, White Masks.* New York: Grove Press, 2008. First published in French in 1952 by Éditions du Seuil.

Fernández Soto, Concha, and Francisco Checa y Olmos. *Los mares de Caronte: Diecisiete calas dramáticas sobre migraciones*. Madrid: Fundamentos, 2016.

Flesler, Daniela. *The Return of the Moor: Spanish Responses to Contemporary Moroccan Immigration*. West Lafayette, Ind.: Purdue University Press, 2008.

Folkart, Jessica A. *Liminal Fiction at the Edge of the Millennium: The Ends of Spanish Identity*. Lewisburg, Pa.: Bucknell University Press, 2014.

Foronda, Luis. "*Mercado libre* o las enfermedades del espíritu humano." In *Mercado Libre*, edited by Luis Araújo, 12–14. Bilbao, Spain: Artezblai, 2008.

Fra-Molinero, Baltasar. "The Suspect Whiteness of Spain." In *At Home and Abroad: Historicizing Twentieth-Century Whiteness in Literature and Performance*, edited by La Vinia Delois Jennings, 147–69. Knoxville: University of Tennessee Press, 2009.

Galán, Ozkar. *Castigat ridendo mores*. In *Los mares de Caronte: diecisiete calas dramáticas sobre migraciones*, edited by Concha Fernández Soto and Francisco Checa y Olmos, 135–49. Madrid: Fundamentos, 2016.

García i Barba, Ignasi. *Amanecer en Orán*. Valladolid, Spain: Caja España, 1996.

García-Manso, Luisa. "Género e inmigración en el teatro español contemporáneo: *Allegro (ma non troppo)* de Carmen Resino." *Estreno* 37, no. 1 (2011): 72–87.

García Márquez, Gabriel. "Señor Presidente." *El País* (Madrid), March 18, 2001, España. https://elpais.com/diario/2001/03/18/espana/984870010_850215.html.

García Orellana, Antonio Daniel. "Eco." In *Mercado libre*, edited by Luis Araújo, 5–9. Bilbao, Spain: Artezblai, 2008.

García Serrano, Rafael. *Eugenio o Proclamación de la primavera*. Madrid: Jerarquía, 1938.

Gómez Glez, Mar. *Cifras*. Madrid: Centro de Documentación Teatral, 2012.

Gordon, Lewis R. *Existentia Africana: Understanding Africana Existential Thought*. New York: Routledge, 2000.

Goytisolo, Juan. *Paisajes después de la batalla*. Barcelona: Montesinos, 1982.

Graham, Helen, and Antonio Sánchez. "The Politics of 1992." In *Spanish Cultural Studies: An Introduction*, edited by Jo Labanyi and Helen Graham, 406–18. Oxford: Oxford University Press, 1995.

Hartman, Saidiya. *Lose Your Mother: A Journey along the Atlantic Slave Route*. New York: Farrar, Straus, and Giroux, 2007.

Heras, Juan Pablo. *Ataque preventivo (puzzle dramático en 31 piezas para 6/8 actores)*. Madrid: Asociación de Autores de Teatro: Consejería de Cultura de la Comunidad de Madrid, 2005.

Hernández Garrido, Raúl. *Despedida*. In *Once voces contra la barbarie del 11-M*, 47–53. Madrid: Fundación Autor, 2006.

Hibernia, Eva. "La carrera." Unpublished manuscript. Last modified October 17, 2017. PDF file.

Ibarra, Esteban. *Los crímenes del odio: Violencia skin y neonazi en españa*. Madrid: Ediciones Temas de Hoy, 2003.

Izquierdo Escribano, Antonio, and Raquel Martínez-Buján. "From Favourites to 'With No Return': Permanence and Mobility of Latin American Immigration in Spain during the 21st Century." *Canadian Ethnic Studies* 46, no. 3 (2014): 103–30.

Jones, Nick. "Cosmetic Ontologies, Cosmetic Subversions: Articulating Black Beauty and Humanity in Luis De Góngora's 'En la fiesta del santísimo sacramento.'" *Journal for Early Modern Cultural Studies* 15, no. 1 (2015): 26–54.

Kleiner-Liebau, Désirée. *Migration and the Construction of National Identity in Spain*. Madrid: Iberoamericana, 2009.

Kunz, Marco. "El drama De la inmigración: *La mirada del hombre oscuro* de Ignacio del Moral y *Ahlán* de Jerónimo López Mozo." In *La inmigración en la literatura española contemporánea*, edited by Irene Andres-Suárez, Marco Kunz, and Inés D'Ors, 215–56. Madrid: Verbum, 2002.

Le Boedec, Guillaume. "Le détroit de Gibraltar: Les limites d'un espace modèle de la lutte européenne contre les migrations irrégulières." *EchoGéo* 2 (2007). https://doi.org/10.4000/echogeo.1488. http://journals.openedition.org/echogeo/1488.

"Ley Orgánica 7/1985, de 1 de julio, sobre derechos y libertades de los extranjeros en España." *Boletín Oficial del Estado* 158 (July 3, 1985): 20824–29.

Lipsyte, Robert. Introduction to *Beyond a Boundary: 50th Anniversary Edition*, edited by C. L. R. James, xvii–xxii. Durham, N.C.: Duke University Press, 2013.

López, Bernabé. "La inmgración de magrebíes y africanos: Asumir la vecindad." In *De la España que emigra a la España que acoge*, edited by A. A. Vigil, A. Asenjo, M. J. Aguilar, and Caballero Fundación Francisco Largo, 480–89. Madrid: Fundación Francisco Largo Caballero, 2006.

López Mozo, Jerónimo. *Ahlán*. Oviedo, Spain: KRK, 2010.

———. *La verdad de los sueños*. In *Obras galardonadas en el V Concurso Iberoamericano de Dramaturgia Infantil*, edited by Jerónimo López Mozo, Jesús del Castillo, and Maxi Rodríguez, 11–44. Bilbao, Spain: Centro de Documentación de las Artes de los Títeres de Bilbao, 2010.

Martín Iniesta, Fernando. *La falsa muerte de Jaro el Negro*. In *Teatro breve entre dos siglos*, edited by Virtudes Serrano, 117–36. Madrid: Cátedra, 2004.

Martin-Márquez, Susan. *Disorientations: Spanish Colonialism in Africa and the Performance of Identity*. New Haven, Conn.: Yale University Press, 2008.

Mbembé, J-A, and Libby Meintjes. "Necropolitics." *Public Culture* 15, no. 1 (2003): 11–40.

Ministerio de Empleo y Seguridad Social (Ministry of Employment and Social Security), Observatorio Permanente de la Inmigración (Permanent Immigration Observatory). *Extranjeros residentes en España: A 30 de junio de 2016*. 2016.

Miralles, Alberto. *Mongo, Boso, Rosco, N'Goe . . . Oniyá*. In *Teatro breve 2*, edited by Alberto Miralles, 95–109. Madrid: Fundamentos, 1999.

Moffette, David. *Governing Irregular Migration: Bordering Culture, Labour, and Security in Spain*. Vancouver: UBC Press, 2018.

Monleón, José. "Prólogo." In *Mercado libre*, edited by Luis Araújo, 9–11. Madrid: Asociación de Autores de Teatro, 2008.

Morejón, Nancy. *Looking Within: Selected Poems, 1954–2000*. Translated by Gabriel Abudu, Mirta Quintanales, Heather Rosario Sievert, David Frye, Kathleen Weaver, and Nancy Abraham Hall. Edited by Juanamaría Cordones-Cook. Detroit: Wayne State University Press, 2003.

Moreno Arenas, José. *El aparcamiento*. In *Trilogías indigestas [I]*, edited by José Moreno Arenas, 163–84. Salobreña, Spain: Alhulia-La Avispa, 2004.

Nair, Parvati. "Europe's 'Last' Wall: Contiguity, Exchange, and Heterotopia in Ceuta, the Confluence of Spain and North Africa." In *Border Interrogations:*

Questioning Spanish Frontiers, edited by Benita Sampedro Vizcaya and Simon Doubleday, 15–41. New York: Bergahn Books, 2008.

The National Security Strategy of the United States of America. Washington, D.C., 2002.

Ngai, Mae M. *Impossible Subjects: Illegal Aliens and the Making of Modern America.* Princeton, N.J.: Princeton University Press, 2004.

Nurse, Keith. "Masculinities in Transition: Gender and the Global Problematique." In *Interrogating Caribbean Masculinities: Theoretical and Empirical Analyses*, edited by Rhoda E. Reddock, 3–37. Kingston, Jamaica: University of the West Indies Press, 2004.

Ortiz de Gondra, Borja. *Mane, Thecel, Phares.* Lleida, Spain: Universitat de Lleida, 2000.

Pallín, Yolanda. *Entrevías.* In *Once voces contra la barbarie del 11-M*, 93–100. Madrid: Fundación Autor, 2006.

Pardellas, Juan Manuel. "El niño polizón que sueña con Messi." *El País* (Madrid), November 17, 2007, España.

Pascual, Itziar. "Un aliento de djembé." In *Friday*, edited by Irma Correa, 7–11. Madrid: Fundación Autor, 2011.

Pérez-Melgosa, Adrián. "Low-Intensity Necropolitics: Slow Violence and Migrant Bodies in Latin American Films." *Arizona Journal of Hispanic Cultural Studies* 20 (2016): 217–36.

Peyró, Josep Pere. *La tanca.* In *Estudis escènics* 36 (2009): 398–408.

Planell, David. "Bazaar." Translated by John Clifford. In *Spanish Plays: New Spanish and Catalan Drama*, edited by Elyse Dodgson and Mary Peate, 105–67. London: Nick Hern Books, 1999.

Primo de Rivera, José Antonio. "Puntos iniciales." *FE*, 1933.

Rengifo Calderón, Álvaro, and Antonio Oporto del Olmo. "Historia, presente y prospectiva de las migraciones en España." *Información comercial española* 826 (2005): 155–66.

Resino, Carmen. *Allegro (ma non troppo).* In *Teatro con múscia*, 167–222. Madrid: Fundamentos, 2008.

———. "Unos pájaros verdes." In *Los mares de Caronte: Diecisiete calas dramáticas sobre migraciones*, edited by Concha Fernández Soto and Francisco Checa y Olmos, 209–20. Madrid: Fundamentos, 2016.

Rius Sant, Xavier. *El libro de la inmigración en España.* Córdoba, Spain: Almuzara, 2007.

Roberts, Neil. *Freedom as Marronage.* Chicago: University of Chicago Press, 2015.

Ross, Catherine B. "¡Mami, Qué Buena Estás! Representations of the Immigrant Woman in *Sobreviviré* (1999) and *I Love You Baby* (2001)." *Letras Femeninas* 34, no. 1 (2008): 217–29.

Salcedo, Hugo. *El viaje de los cantores.* Toluca: Universidad Autónoma del Estado de México, 2014.

Saldo migratorio con el extranjero por año, país de nacimiento y nacionalidad (española/extranjera). Instituto Nacional de Estadística (National Institute of Statistics), Spain. http://www.ine.es/jaxiT3/Tabla.htm?t=24310&L=0.

Sampedro Vizcaya, Benita, and Simon R. Doubleday. *Border Interrogations: Questioning Spanish Frontiers.* New York: Berghahn Books, 2008.

Sharpe, Christina. *In the Wake: On Blackness and Being*. Durham, N.C.: Duke University Press, 2016.

Simón, Ana Iris. "Pasé una noche con los lateros del centro de Madrid." *Vice*, August 15, 2017. https://www.vice.com/es/article/599pdb/noche-lateros-madrid.

Sontag, Susan. *Regarding the Pain of Others*. New York: Farrar, Straus and Giroux, 2003.

Stevens, Camilla. "Encuentros culturales: La parodia postcolonialista en *la isla amarilla* y *la mirada del hombre oscuro*." In *Entre actos: diálogos sobre teatro español entre siglos*, edited by Martha T. Halsey and Phyllis Zatlin. University Park, Pa.: Estreno Plays, 1999.

Toasije, Antumi. "The Africanity of Spain: Identity and Problematization." *Journal of Black Studies* 39, no. 3 (2009): 348–55.

Torrado, Vicente. "La inmigración latinoamericana en España." *Departamento de Asuntos Económicos y Sociales. Organización de las Naciones Unidas* (2006).

"Tráfico humano: 18 mexicanos muertos al intentar pasar a E.U." *La Jornada*, July 3, 1987, 1.

Vega-Durán, Raquel. *Emigrant Dreams, Immigrant Borders: Migrants, Transnational Encounters, and Identity in Spain*. Blue Ridge Summit, Pa.: Bucknell University Press, 2016.

Zantop, Susanne. *Colonial Fantasies: Conquest, Family, and Nation in Precolonial Germany, 1770–1870*. Durham, N.C.: Duke University Press, 1997.

Zapata-Barrero, Ricard. "The Muslim Community and Spanish Tradition: Maurophobia as a Fact, and Impartiality as a Desideratum." In *Multiculturalism, Muslims and Citizenship: A European Approach*, edited by Tariq Modood, Anna Triandafyllidou, and Ricard Zapata-Barrero, 143–61. New York: Routledge, 2006.

INDEX